HOW TO MAKE MONEY IN REAL ESTATE

HOW TO MAKE MONEY IN REAL ESTATE

INVESTING ▲ RENTING ▲ SELLING BUYING ▲ CONDOS ▲ RAW LAND ▲ LEASING ▲ COOPS ▲ SHELTERS ▲ RESIDENTIAL ▲ COMMERCIAL ▲

BY STEVEN JAMES LEE

BOARDROOM® BOOKS
500 Fifth Avenue, New York, New York 10110

$50

This book is dedicated to my friend and wife, Karen, who understands that the thing that counts is not what we could do but what we actually do.

Second Printing

Library of Congress Cataloging in Publication Data

Lee, Steven James.

How to Make Money in Real Estate.

Includes index.
1. Real estate investment. I. Title.
HD1382.5.L43 332.63'24 81-3868
ISBN 0-932648-19-3 AACR2

Table of Contents

CHAPTER ONE

Your Financial Future

Real estate investment is a specialized art that can confuse even relatively sophisticated individuals. It has so many options and so many methods that it appears easiest to dismiss real estate as too risky or too complex for the nonprofessional investor. Looking at the literature on real estate in any bookstore, one sees literally dozens of books about how to make millions in one year in your spare time through real estate manipulation. All of these promises are basically just that--promises. The truth is that conservative real estate investment is the slow and steady way to create and build wealth. It doesn't happen overnight; further, there is some effort required in the management of your portfolio.

Why should real estate be the cornerstone of a conservative executive investment program? The attractive feature of real estate is that it is a tangible item in a world likely to continue to undergo sustained inflation. To dramatize the point, let's take a simple example. According to the Health Insurance Institute, the value of the human body in 1980 is $7.28, compared to a mere 98 cents just ten years ago. So while you may feel older, be assured that your makeup of calcium, potassium, sodium, and trace elements has increased a whopping 643 percent during the past decade.

Buildings are very much like your body. They are formed from hundreds of different components that come together to form a functional unit. There are electrical systems, heating and cooling systems, support systems, and space systems, all with many individual parts. The cost of these many parts, while inflation lasts, is on an upward spiral. True, as a building ages, some parts wear out. This partially explains why the value of older structures does not go up in exact proportion to the increasing cost of new construction. But if you took the effort to compare costs for such items as nails, wood, concrete, and electrical fixtures over the last decade, the increase would be very substantial. What this means to you as an investor is that your real estate holdings are designed to be a store of value in goods and services.

Note, however, that the analogy is not exact. There are many outside factors that affect real estate values. For example, neighborhoods can change and cause prices to decline (or increase) dramatically; new and better building technology can render older structures obsolete; and new laws, with changed tax and rental implications, can alter the profit expectations of the otherwise free market for properties. Thus, replacement cost of physical items is not an absolute assurance of value.

Higher oil and energy prices seem here to stay. The United States, along with other industrial nations, has chosen to accommodate the huge increase in energy costs by spreading inflation throughout the economy. Inflation has become a structural problem. Individuals and businesses have become conditioned by the expectation of inflation. Government anti-inflation efforts may cause a temporary downturn in inflation, but the standard remedies are not likely to cure it while the underlying causes remain intact. It is against this background that you should examine what real estate is likely to mean to the long-range goal of building wealth.

Analyzing your assets

Most executives do not have the foggiest idea of what they are worth when their assets are compared to their liabilities. Worse yet, they have paid little attention to building up their net worth during their working lifetime. There is a real danger of a rude awakening at the time of retirement. Suddenly the salary income stops, and there is a dramatic drop in the standard of living to accommodate the modest amounts of income generated from a pension. Start planning now to avoid this tragedy.

First, let us discuss the value of savings. Savings should mean not only funds deposited into an account in a commercial bank but also the diversion of a portion of after-tax income into a capital pool that will grow. To understand this more precisely, look at the time line in Figure 1.1.

Figure 1.1

Time Line

Period 1	Period 2	Period X
Now Present Value		Future Value

Each dollar of income placed in your capital pool has a present value at the moment it is available for investment, and a greater future value at the end of an investment period. The time line above commences with a present value, shows increases in value during each succeeding period, and ends at some fixed date with a much larger future value. So money invested at a present value builds up a capital pool as it grows into a larger future value along the time line. Dollars that are earned and immediately spent never have a chance to attain a future value.

No competent executive would run a company without adequate provision for its growth and ability to meet its liabilities. Think of retirement, with the loss of a major portion of income, as a future liability. There must be adequate reserves to take up the slack and maintain the smooth operation of the family. Savings are the key to such reserves, and it is impossible to achieve security without them. Therefore, you should form and maintain your capital pool immediately if you have not yet focused on building net worth. A reasonable guideline is the diversion of 10 percent to 30 percent of net income into a capital pool that remains untouched during the time line of your active employment.

Some executives have various investments they stumbled into during the course of their careers. For many, their single largest asset is already a real estate holding. That is the ownership of their single family home. In other cases, there are stock options, actual stock, insurance policies, annuities, and a wide range of corporate financial "perks" that come with elevated positions of responsibility. Sorting through this maze to arrive at a clear personal net worth is the beginning step toward taking advantage of the opportunities in real estate.

Worksheet One is an excellent format for computing your net worth. It is not as simple an exercise as you might imagine. However, real estate is an investment predicated on a combination of equity and debt– the larger the equity, the larger the debt and the more substantial the size of the real estate ventures open to you. As we shall see later, the more sophisticated types of financing techniques require relatively large projects to make the effort worthwhile. If you want to relate these techniques to your own financial situation, you should complete Worksheet One before going on with this book.

WORKSHEET ONE

Personal Financial Statement

This is a statement of my financial condition as of the ________day of ______, 19__.

Assets		Liabilities	
Cash (Schedule A)	$______	Notes Payable Banks (Schedule A)	$______
Stocks and Bonds (Schedule B)	______	Notes Payable to Relatives	______
Accounts and Notes Receivable:	______	Notes Payable to Others	______
Due from relatives and friends	______	Accounts Payable	______
Due from others--good	______	Federal & State Income Taxes Payable	______
Doubtful	______	Other Accrued Taxes & Interest	______
Real Estate Owned (Schedule C)	______	Mortgages Payable (Schedule C)	______
Mortgages Owned (Schedule D)	______	Installment Contracts Payable	______
Cash Surrender Value Life Insurance (Schedule E)	______	Other Liabilities (including credit card, revolving credit and charge acounts) itemize:	______
Other assets (itemize):			
Total Assets	$______	TOTAL LIABILITIES	$______
		NET WORTH	$______

Schedule A

Cash Balances and Bank Loans

	Statement Date	
Name of Bank	Cash Balance	Amount Owing
Cash on Hand		
TOTALS AS PER STATEMENT		

Schedule B

Stocks and Bonds

Shares or Bonds	Name of Security	In Name of	Present Market Value
	U.S. Governments, series		
	Municipal Bonds		
	Corporate Bonds		
	Stocks		

Schedule C

Real Estate Owned

Location, Type of Property and Date Acquired	Title in Name of	Cost	Recent Appraised Value	Mortgage Amount Due

Schedule D

Real Estate Mortgages Owned

Type of Lien (1st, 2nd, 3rd, etc.) Location and Type of Property	Mortgagee of Record	Original Amount	Present Amount	Maturity

Schedule E

Life Insurance

Face Amount	Name of Company	Beneficiary	Type of Policy	Cash Value	Loans Against Policy

The inflation imperative

It used to be an accepted rule that what goes up must come down. The new inflation imperative is: what goes up comes down a little and then goes up higher still. We have spoken about inflation, but here we shall examine its real impact on individuals and their investment options. If you accept our conclusion from above that inflation will continue as an unrelenting fact of life, then you are in agreement with most financial experts.

Let us look at a variety of investments during the period from 1967 through 1977 in constant 1967 dollars. We will choose this period because it had a fairly predictable inflation rate around the 5 to 6.6 percentage range. The violent price explosions of 1978-1980 may or may not continue, but inclusion of those years would skew up our values from the relatively consistent increases in values of 1967-1977. If you are of the opinion that the wider swings of the 1978-1980 period will be the wave of the future, simply amplify our examples to derive the more exaggerated price structure you foresee. We shall consider what impact inflation had on investments in a more modest period, which is apt to be the minimum expectation of most officials.

During the 1967 to 1977 period one of the most worthwhile investments was home ownership. If you had invested $10,000 in 1967 in a home, at the end of the ten year period your investment would have been worth $11,830 in 1967 constant dollars. Thus you would not have lost ground to inflation; in fact, you would have gained. In addition to the long-term gain in value, the homeowner would have achieved favorable income tax deductions for interest payments on his mortgage and all local property and school taxes.

For those investing in real property other than a house, the situation was very similar. A $10,000 investment in an office building during the 1967-1977 period was worth $11,990 in constant 1967 dollars. A $10,000 investment in a farm during the 1967-1977 period became worth $15,570 in constant 1967 dollars, according to the U.S. Department of Commerce. Raw land in the United States, depending on the region and location in its particular area, increased on average by an amount slightly less than farm properties.

But what of the investment alternatives? Over the years a large number of experts have cited the common stocks of well-managed companies as a dependable hedge against inflation. The dogma is that such companies will boost their earnings and dividends over time and that public shares will increase in value as a reflection of this trend. The Dow-Jones industrial average is composed of 30 blue-chip companies that represent the very cream of American industry. The Dow-Jones industrial average stood at about 800 in 1966, and even in 1980 was around the same level. On that basis, the stock investor has surely lost ground to inflation. Looking at the 1967-1977 period for a broader stock market average, the $10,000 investment in common stocks (assuming reinvestment of dividends) would have been worth only $7,070 in constant 1967 dollars in 1977. Of course, there were individual corporate winners during the period that far outpaced inflation. But on the whole, stocks were a poor hedge.

Corporate bonds fared pretty well between 1967-1977. A $10,000 investment was worth $10,420 in 1977 in constant 1967 dollars. However, if we follow that story through the turmoil of 1978-1980, the value of corporate bonds plunged as inflation pushed interest rates up to historic highs. The safe and reliable income investments lost significant value to investors who had to sell them during the peak interest rate periods. The millions of Americans who owned U.S. Government Series E savings bonds did much worse. They were stuck with a relatively long-term, illiquid investment that did not return even half the income lost by high inflation rates.

For over 15 years, money kept in savings accounts has not kept pace with the inflation rate. In the period from 1967-1977 a $10,000 deposit in your local savings bank earned 5 to 5¼ percent. Thus in 1977 it was worth $9,410 in constant 1967 dollars. The principal benefit of a savings account was, and is, its safety. Today, however, there are money market funds that pay much better rates to the small investor and still offer a high degree of safety. But don't expect to do much better than keep even with the long-run loss of your purchasing power.

There is a diversity of other investments that did well during the inflation of 1967-1977, ranging from works of art and antique furniture through stamps and coins or precious stones. The main problem there is that the expertise required to choose wisely is beyond the grasp of most laymen. This means you are relying for the most part on the opinions of others for the price you pay for the investment and the price at which it is sold. There is also the disadvantage of special insurance coverage and, in many cases, bank vault storage. The resale market is somewhat illiquid--if things go wrong, it may even be nonexistent.

There is another important dimension to the inflation imperative as it affects individuals. That is the tax implication of increasing income during a period of sustained inflation. In 1967 the average taxpayer paid out just over 14 percent of his income in federal taxes. For 1980 the rate is closer to 19 percent and is likely to rise throughout the next decade. These rate increases continue in spite of repeated and substantial tax breaks and reductions. Our problem is the bracket system that taxes marginal income at higher and higher rates. The U.S. has not adopted the Canadian system of tax indexing, which automatically lowers rates to offset increases in the consumer price index. You seem to earn more, but it is really substantially offset by the increased skimming done by the government.

Where does this leave the conservative investor? With a strong reason to look hard at the real estate market. Not only will it help him keep up with inflation, but there are tax shelter aspects to mitigate the effects of increasing tax burdens.

Risk for a conservative investor

Risk means that you are prepared to lose some or all of your money in return for a potential profit. The only truly riskless way of keeping money is in the form of cash. But in the inflationary environment outlined above, the erosion of purchasing power would eventually make those idle cash dollars almost worthless. Therefore, we must learn to deal with risk on terms that appear comfortable. Never extend yourself beyond the limits of reasonable prudence. These limits, which we shall define, delineate the conservative investor.

For the purposes of staking out some boundaries to guide us in an investment strategy, let us say there are three levels of investment risk. The lowest level seeks maximum security of the principal sum invested and a fixed rate of return that is fairly certain. The medium level puts less than half of the principal invested at any foreseeable risk and seeks some capital appreciation as well as a rate of return. High risk investment holds a clear possibility of losing the entire principal investment, or, conversely, the potential for large gains in capital appreciation.

When you have arrived at your net worth figure you can make some calculated judgments about how much risk you can afford relative to your income group. One standard formula is to multiply $1,000 times your age to arrive at a relatively fast track salary. If you are significantly above, you can afford more risk because you have the ability to recover quickly from a poor investment. Conversely, if you are at or below your age target it is probably wise to be more conservative in your judgment.

It is also wise to consider your occupation and the likelihood of future salary advances. If you are in a corporate environment, realistically appraise your chances of advancement. A glance at the size and susceptibility of your employer to adverse economic conditions is also appropriate. Your seniority level means little if the fundamental business could disappear, interrupting the income on which you and your family depend.

Although any guidelines are subjective, we can make some generalizations in associating risk with net worth and age. There are two helpful calculations for the individual, but they will be influenced by your goals and temperament. The first rule is that an excellent capital pool is $20,000 times the number of years you have worked at your profession; a good capital pool is $10,000 times the years worked; and an average capital pool is $5,000 times the years you have worked. The second calculation is that the maximum high risk exposure of your capital pool relative to your age should be no more than 100 minus your age. These thumbnail guidelines are summarized in Figure 1.2, with the assumption that an individual commences working at age 25 and will retire at age 65.

Figure 1.2

Age	Years Worked	Years Until Retirement	Excellent Capital Pool	Good Capital Pool	Average Capital Pool	Maximum High Risk
25	0	40	--	--	--	75%
30	5	35	$100,000	$ 50,000	$ 25,000	70%
35	10	30	200,000	100,000	50,000	65%
40	15	25	300,000	150,000	75,000	60%
45	20	20	400,000	200,000	100,000	55%
50	25	15	500,000	250,000	125,000	50%
55	30	10	600,000	300,000	150,000	45%
60	35	5	700,000	350,000	175,000	40%
65	40	0	800,000	400,000	200,000	35%

Distribution of investments

Diversity in investments is a sound policy. The concept is based on the assumption that it is very unlikely that everything will turn sour at the same time. You should probably have an overall portfolio that is divided into several areas of opportunity. Real estate may be the foundation, but stocks, bonds, certificates of deposit, antiques, paintings, gold, silver, and gems are also potentially profitable. They could be roaring ahead in times when real estate is in the low ebb of its cycle.

This leaves us to deal with a basic question. How much of your available capital pool should be committed to real estate investments? The answer involves a great deal of subjective judgment on your part. Time is the underlying ingredient in conservative real estate investing, and it is beyond the control of the investor. Because of this, the amount of your overall investment portfolio committed to real estate is somewhat correlative with your age. We add to this two other facts about growing older. First, it is wise to leave your estate highly liquid to provide for taxes and distributions to your heirs. Secondly, as you grow older it is likely that you will want passive investments that require as little attention as possible. Real estate in general is not liquid and almost always needs personal attention and management. Therefore, Figure 1.3 sets forth some general guidelines as to the percentage of capital pool that should be in real estate at various ages.

Figure 1.3

Age in Years	Real Estate Portion of Capital
25	65%-100%
30	65%-90%
35	65%-75%
40	65%-75%
45	50%-75%
50	50%-60%
55	35%-50%
60	25%-35%

Note that in your early working years a substantial portion of your capital pool should be in real estate. That is because a basic part of conservative investing is taking advantage of tax incentives that encourage the placement of capital in specific investments. There is probably no single investment with more individual tax benefits and government support than owning your own residence. The attractive yearly deductions, coupled with the provision for deferral of gains on sale, are the cornerstone of building a net worth. Therefore, the first investment should be your own residence, whether cooperative, condominium, town house, or single family home. Since most people don't start out with a large capital base, it is certainly permissible in the early years to deploy most or all of your capital in the down payment.

In money management advice there is an almost universally accepted rule: it is essential to maintain an instantly available cash reserve to meet current living costs. Experts differ as to an exact amount, but it is fairly safe to have four months of living expenses in passbook savings accounts. This money is not part of your capital pool. It is strictly an emergency fund to meet the costs of illness or other unforeseen disaster.

Real estate outlook

The outlook is very bright for real estate markets in the United States during the coming decade. Many experts believe we are at the midpoint of the longest period of sustained real estate growth in American history. Perhaps one of the reasons for this is that on the whole, investments in real property have matched or exceeded the inflation rate. Thus, a considerable amount of capital is readily available for real estate projects of all types.

Supply and demand for housing units are clearly not in tune. The demand for new housing units will be 2.3 million annually through 1985, while the units currently being constructed do not come close to reaching this amount. High interest rates dampen enthusiasm for building new housing, and also raise monthly mortgage costs beyond the means of a great many potential purchasers. In addition, rents have failed to rise in proportion to costs (in some areas because of rent control) and this has forced many developers out of multifamily rental construction because the returns are unattractive. It is likely that housing supplies will be tight for a sustained period until the shortfall is corrected. When demand cannot be met by the available supply it means rising prices. This is usually good news for the real estate investor.

It is predicted that new office construction in many areas of the country will rival the 1968-1972 surge for the first five years of the decade. Development is likely to be strongest in the larger central business districts where mass transit is available, since the energy crisis has brought real estate investors away from the concept of remote office parks situated on cheaper land in the suburbs. Office supply and demand are pretty well in balance at the present time. Therefore, vacancy factors are low and landlords are enjoying a good return on their investment.

The number of new super-regional shopping centers is predicted to drop dramatically. This may present great opportunities to buy and upgrade older but well-located houses and commercial buildings. The idea of buying an older strip shopping building, or even a shopping center, and remodeling it will become more appealing. As business and commerce begin to refocus on the urban areas, many declining residential areas will reverse their trend and become attractive investments.

In the past, hotel and motel rates have managed to outpace inflation. However, there are some doubts as to whether this type of investment will continue to be attractive. Construction costs have grown to the point that new development may be much more risky. In addition, rising fuel costs will force up plane fares and may curtail a lot of vacation travel. Present rates may also be near their high, so that the potential for nearly instantaneous adjustment in pricing structure for hotel and motel rooms may stop.

Overall, the future of real estate in the first half of the new decade is rosy. There is a smorgasbord of opportunities available to suit the needs of the executive who desires a conservative investment with a likelihood of capital growth. The rest of this book will focus on the specifics that will prepare an individual to direct his own, and in some cases his company's, capital pool into potentially profitable ventures.

CHAPTER TWO

An Overview of Real Estate Investment

If you are convinced that real estate could be good for you and your money, then this is the right place for a broad overview. The following material will explain some real property investments that are suitable for the conservative investor. Some of these areas will be covered in more detail in subsequent discussions. In this chapter the entire picture is presented so that our later discussions can be individually framed in their proper perspective.

Before we go to specific types of investments, let's address ourselves to two issues that affect all of them. First, leverage and its positive and negative attributes is worth some mention. The concept of leverage is simply that an investor attempts to control a relatively large amount of assets with a comparatively small equity investment. For example, a building costs $1,000,000 and is purchased with a $950,000 mortgage.

The ratio of the asset to equity investment is $1,000,000 ÷ $50,000, or 20 to 1. If real estate values in the area go up 10 percent in a year, the investor will realize a profit of $100,000 (.10 × 1,000,000) if the building is sold and there are no selling expenses. That is a fabulous return of 200 percent on invested equity.

That's the plus side of leverage. There is a negative side that is often overlooked. If the $950,000 mortgage is a floating-rate loan and interest rates skyrocket, the investor can be wiped out. A floating rate means that the loan is set at a fixed percentage rate above the prime rate of commercial banks. Let's say that when the mortgage was obtained it was negotiated at the prime rate plus 3 percentage points. At the time, the prime rate was eight percent, so interest on the loan was 11 percent of $104,500 per year. After all expenses for operation (such as taxes, fuel, maintenance, and vacancy) there was an income of $5,000 from the property, giving the investor a 10 percent cash on cash return ($5,000/$50,000). That seemed nice and comfortable at the time it was negotiated.

All of a sudden, in 1979 the government determined it would pursue a policy whereby the Federal Reserve drove up interest rates to record levels. Our 20-to-1 leveraged investor gets a call from his bank that the prime rate has just risen to 19½ percent. This means the interest rate on his loan is now 22½ percent or $213,750 per year (.225 times $950,000). The difference between initial interest charges of $104,500 and the new interest charge of $213,750 is $109,250 per year. Against this the investor can apply only $5,000 of excess income. To make matters worse, the building cannot be sold because mortgages are just not available. Our investor must come up with $104,250 of additional cash each year! The squeeze is on and the negatives of leverage are likely to wipe out the investment. If the investor personally guaranteed the loan, all of his assets may be wiped out.

There is no hard and fast rule about how much leverage is wise. It depends on the scope of all your assets and how they are deployed. Another factor is how long you intend to hold the investment. The longer the holding period the more factors that are beyond your control--such as a sharp rise in interest rates. On the other hand, a quick sale, as we will discuss later, has certain disadvantageous tax consequences. Our conclusion on leverage: the conservative investor must have the reserve staying power to meet the worst. He can hold on through the storm clouds of the cycle and wait to sell at a more advantageous time.

The second broad concept in real estate investment is the balance between the chance for capital growth and income. Age is one factor here. In general, the younger investor should be more interested in capital growth than income. Our time line from Chapter One (see page 3) reminds us that it is best to strive for the largest capital pool possible at the youngest age. On the other hand, responsibilities and the need for liquidity must weigh on this decision. If you support several people, some of whom are ill or are likely to need extensive care, then it may be important to invest in income-producing property. Raw land, which produces nothing in income, and may even have a negative cash flow for tax expenses, might only prove a burden. And the sale of raw land may be difficult under the gun.

Income level is another factor in choosing between capital growth and income from real estate. If you are in a very high tax bracket perhaps you don't want more income. True, real estate generally shelters most of its income from adverse tax consequences, but even so there may be some flow that cannot be sheltered. The solution here might be projects designed for long-term growth of value rather than income. The increased value will not be a taxable event until the property is sold. Even then, some advantageous tax rules could further delay payment of taxes.

Owner-occupied real estate

American tax law has built up a long series of rules that make home ownership very advantageous. The owner-occupied home has one characteristic unique to the real estate investment world. If you are over the age of 55, the tax laws allow you to exclude from your tax return up to $125,000 of realized gain on the sale of your principal residence. You must have occupied the house for at least three of the five years preceding the sale in order to qualify, and this exclusion may only be used once in a lifetime. Still, can you think of any other investment you can enjoy daily, supervise easily, sell for a profit, and keep the first $125,000 of gain out of the clutches of the IRS?

In addition to special tax breaks, the owner-occupied home has the normal benefits of real estate. Interest on mortgage payments and property taxes are deductible on your itemized federal tax return. If you rent, these deductions are not available to you. All permanent repairs and improvements are added to your cost basis when you sell. Thus, taxes due are calculated on the difference between your adjusted basis (purchase price plus repairs and improvements) and the actual selling price. Even so, any gain on the sale of a residence owned for more than a year is taxed at the favorable rates associated with long-term capital gains.

Of course, your family residence is more than a real estate investment. It is located in a particular community that probably appeals to your family. And when your property appreciates (as it doubtless has) and is sold, some interesting things happen. If you buy another principal residence within two years that costs more than the house you sold, you pay no taxes on the gain. If you build a new house that costs more than the one you sold (not hard in today's climate), you still have a two year grace period. Such a transfer may free a lot of capital for alternative investment. For example, in 1976 you bought a house for $80,000 that has a current market value of $180,000. A local bank will give you a 75 percent mortgage on a $200,000 house in the same area. If you make the swap, you only have to put up $50,000 in equity for your new house. You probably have $125,000 of equity in your old house if you look at its current market value and your original down payment and mortgage principal payments. That means that you will have about $75,000 available for other conservative real estate investment. Right now that money just sits there doing nothing.

There are some other angles to this family residence game. If you are a veteran, you may be able to obtain a favorable interest rate and a low down payment mortgage. There is also the Federal Housing Administration, which insures mortgages with down payments as low as three percent of the purchase price. These advantages generally prevail with lower-priced houses, but that may not be entirely bad. If you are over 55 and your children are out on their own, maybe it's time to think about a smaller house. The VA and FHA vary as to how much red tape is involved, but on the whole it is more than with conventional lenders.

Investment in a residence does not produce any cash flow or depreciation deduction. Its primary purpose as an investment vehicle is in appreciation of value. Thus, if you can speed up the increase in value, and then move, you are much better off. One of the best ways to accomplish this is to buy an older house that can be made more modern and comfortable. If you are somewhat handy, then you have an excellent opportunity to build a nice capital pool very quickly. In family residences, the kitchens, family rooms, and bathrooms are the most important selling features. Look for a well-located house with a modest kitchen separated by a wall from a butler's pantry. Remove that wall, spruce up the cabinets or buy new ones, add a nice floor--you have a modern eat-in kitchen. That adds enormous value to an older house. Some painting and other decorating thrown on top of this produces a resale candidate. The more labor you do yourself, of course, the greater the profit.

Another quick fix on a house is the creation of a year-round family room from a screened porch. There is a large selection of sliding glass doors that can replace the screens. They are easy to install and almost any do-it-yourselfer can do an excellent job with little inconvenience to the family.

For young couples, fixing up older houses can be fun as well as financially rewarding. There are books to tell you how to do everything you are likely to attempt. They are easy to read, and the work is not that difficult or demanding. You can do all of these things. And if you get stuck, ask a professional for advice. They are likely to be very helpful.

The work is good exercise and the knowledge you acquire will prove useful all your life. Lest you dismiss this suggestion lightly, the facts are that many millionaires made some real money just this way. Meanwhile they held down an executive position for the cash coming in from a regular salary. Renovating older houses is not for everybody, but for many it can provide the base capital and construction knowledge basic to other real estate investment.

Raw land speculation

Whoever said that people should buy land because it's in fixed supply missed the boat. Land in the wilderness of Alaska, when and if it can be sold, is priced at around $10 an acre. In midtown New York City a square block can cost $100,000,000. What this tells you is that no one is likely to build the Empire State Building where the deer and the antelope play. Thus we come to the three basic rules of raw land speculation. The first, second, and third rules are location, location, and location. You may have heard this before. It's true.

It is likely that if you buy raw land today it will appreciate in value. However, the fact that you receive more for the land when it is resold does not mean that you made a good investment. It does not even mean that you have made much of a profit. For example, let us say that you purchase 10 acres of land for $50,000 cash. That land has a carrying cost each year of $1,000 in taxes and an opportunity cost of $3,500 per year, figured as the seven percent you could have earned passively in a high grade corporate bond after all taxes. We will also assume that brokerage and other costs of the transaction average around eight percent for the buy and for the subsequent resale.

Another way to account for the seven percent per year we could have earned is to use the present value of the price we get on resale. Present value is how much a specific amount of money, received at a point in the future, is worth today, assuming a set interest rate throughout the period. Let us say we will sell the land at $75,000 five years from now. Therefore we want to know the present value of $75,000 to be received in five years, assuming the minimum breakeven desired is the seven percent we could receive passively from a high grade corporate bond. Using present value tables or a calculator, we can calculate that the present value of $75,000 to be received in five years if an interest rate of seven percent is assumed, is $53,473. Or, in reverse, $53,473 invested at seven percent for five years with reinvestment of interest would accumulate to $75,000.

But this is not the end of our calculation. We must also allow for our yearly expenses on raw land. Figure 2.1, below, shows a time line on our investment.

Figure 2.1

Time Line

Year 0	Year 1	Year 2	Year 3	Year 4	Year 5
$50,000 + 4,000 brokerage					
$54,000	$1,000 tax	$1,000 tax	$1,000 tax	$1,000 tax	$1,000 tax
					75,000 - 6,000 brokerage
					$69,000

Our present value figure of $53,473 does not take into account the yearly payment of taxes at $1,000 per year nor the eight percent brokerage fee paid on purchase and sale ($4,000 and $6,000, respectively). In year 0 we actually invested $54,000 cash when we total $50,000 for the land plus

$4,000 for brokerage. In years 1 through 5 we invest $1,000 each year in taxes and this money, by our assumption, could also have been earning at seven percent in a high-grade corporate bond. In year 5 we also invested $6,000 in a brokerage fee when we received the $75,000 selling price; thus, we received only $69,000 from the investment.

Boiling this down with a calculator, we want to know what net present value of money we would have to invest, with the flows of further investments in years 1 through 5, to end up with $69,000 at the end of year 5. The required sum of money would come out to be $45,808, clearly less than the $54,000 cash we lay out at the purchase date. The raw land bought in this transaction is a raw deal when compared to seven percent high-grade bonds available at each investment period.

Office buildings

There is no question that a good office building at its prime is better than a good apartment building. The commercial tenant does not disturb his landlord on holidays to repair toilets. An office renter only uses the building from 9 a.m. until 5 p.m. on weekdays. In addition, there are no rent controls available to commercial tenants; thus, the termination of a lease is a time for glee. The rent can be raised to whatever the market will bear for the renewing or new tenant.

But the average office building is a much larger investment than an apartment building. For one thing, there are a limited number of locations with the right access to public transportation and other businesses. This means that the land under an office building costs substantially more than the land under most residential structures. To take full advantage of land

and location, an office building needs to have a lot of square footage. This means a taller building and its associated higher construction costs for such things as elevators, heating and cooling, and steel framing.

Management of an office building is also more complex than management of an apartment. Tenants must be creditworthy in relation to the amount of space they wish to take. If the renter of half the net rentable area goes bust, the building may suddenly be in trouble. In an apartment house, on the other hand, no single tenant contributes that substantially to the overall rental base. The tenant mix of businesses is also quite important. Quality tenants in highly visible locations will attract other such tenants. Conversely, a second-rate business tenant may make a preferred tenant think twice at lease renewal time. Management of energy for heating and cooling also becomes a critical factor in operating expense. Failure to keep careful control of such systems can severely impact cash flow. Finally, elevators have to be properly serviced at a reasonable cost.

Demand for office space is more subject to the vagaries of the business cycle than is demand for housing. A weak market for office space can cause a severe downturn in income, since most expenses are relatively constant. The owner must be financially equipped to ride out the cycle rather than settling for inferior tenants or curtailed services. In residential real estate the landlord takes comfort in the fact that people have to live somewhere. Even in a severe downward cycle the landlord of a residential property can probably sign six-month leases at reduced rates. The commercial lease, due to the high cost of tenant improvements, is generally for a longer period. The landlord can be locked in at the reduced rate long after the business cycle has turned and demand has improved.

Another problem with office buildings is obsolescence. People find old apartments charming. Business finds old space unprofitable or impractical. When the age of the building forces a loss of profit or image, the first class tenants will move. Thus, an office building requires constant maintenance and upgrading. The space must be kept desirable or else there will be a rapid changeover in the prestige of the building that will directly affect its bottom line.

Vacation homes

The main reason for buying a vacation home is to cut down the cost of family vacations. A secondary motive can be the possible appreciation of the real estate as an offset to operating expenses. When fuel was cheap, people were solidly convinced that distance was not a factor in the real estate value of a vacation bungalow. Today, if you have a camel, distance is still not a factor. For the rest of us, it is wise to choose a vacation home that is within round trip range of a single tank of gas from a major population center. Even so, appreciation is likely to be slower than in the preenergy crisis heyday.

There are some tax rules that can help you cut down on the cost of a vacation home by renting it part or most of the time. If you rent out your vacation home for 14 or fewer days each year, and you use it the rest of the time, the IRS does not require you to report any rental income. So if July 4th week, Labor Day week, Christmas week, or Easter week are very big in the area in which you vacation, consider collecting tax-free the premium rents these special weeks will command. It might offset half or more of your yearly upkeep expenses.

What if you want to rent the house almost all year and use it yourself only a couple of weeks? The person asking that question wants to use his vacation home as a tax shelter to offset other income. If that is the case then you must treat your vacation home strictly as a real estate business. You cannot use the house more than 14 days each year or more than 10 percent of the time it is actually rented during the year. Then you can deduct mortgage interest, taxes, rental costs, insurance, and depreciation. Let us look at a specific case. You buy a $75,000 vacation home with a 10 percent interest rate on a mortgage principal of $60,000. Real estate taxes are $2,000, insurance costs $500, and rental costs are another $500 for ads in the local newspaper or for a local broker. The value of the house apart from the land is $60,000 and you elect to use straight line depreciation on a 30-year life, which then allows you to take $2,000 of depreciation deduction each year. Figure 2.2 shows the bottom line cost for a taxpayer in the 50 percent bracket.

Figure 2.2

Bottom Line Costs

	Total Personal Use	Split Use	Total Rental
Mortgage Interest	$6,000	$6,000	$6,000
Insurance	500	500	500
Real Estate Taxes	2,000	2,000	2,000
Rental Expense	0	500	500
Cash Expenses	$8,500	$9,000	$9,000
Depreciation	0	0	2,000
Total Expenses	$8,500	$9,000	$11,000

If you can only rent out the property for $7,000 per year in the split use category, that is the most you may deduct for mortgage interest and taxes even though they cost you $8,000. If it is a total rental (remember you can use it up to 14 days each year), then $11,000 is available as a deduction even though cash outlays were only $9,000.

When you sell the vacation house any appreciation in value is a capital gain and subject to taxes. This is not your primary residence, so gain cannot be postponed by rolling it over into another house. The vacation house does not qualify for the once-in-a-lifetime $100,000 exclusion for owners over the age of 55. Any depreciation taken over the years will be recaptured in the sale. This is done by subtracting the total amount of depreciation from your cost basis. For example, if we sell our $75,000 vacation home five years later for $100,000, our cost basis will be $65,000 ($75,000 minus 5 × $2,000). Our calculation of capital gains will then be on the difference between $100,000 and $65,000, or $35,000 subject to taxes.

Apartment houses

America is not building enough housing to meet the demands of its growing and changing population. During periods of high interest rates new apartment construction is all but stopped. This is largely because construction loans are generally floating rate loans at three percent to six percent over the prime rate. When the prime rate is 19½ percent, as it was in 1980, that is very expensive money indeed. A delay at the construction site due to nondelivery of materials, labor unrest, bad weather, or some other factor beyond the developer's control can easily bankrupt a new project. Additions to the apartment housing stock will probably not catch up with the generally strong demand. Therefore, the present owners of apartment dwellings should look forward to improvement in profitability of their holdings as well as appreciation in values.

To investors new in the marketplace the picture is not so rosy. Purchasing an existing apartment building will mean paying top dollar to the seller. There will also be little opportunity to get favorable contractual provisions--a second mortgage, for example. Still, there are certain real estate categories within the apartment area that may be more advantageous investments. One is picking up an older building, renovating it so the apartment rents can be raised substantially, and selling the building with the larger rent roll. This works for townhouse developments as well as for high rise apartments. Another is the concept of buying a poorly managed complex and reducing operating costs substantially by proper management. This can include adding new energy systems or modernizing with better insulation and more efficient equipment. It can also include reducing the vacancy rate, reducing staff, and shortening leases on renewal so that future costs can be passed on more readily.

Abandon any plans to purchase apartment properties in localities with rent control laws. It is almost impossible to come out whole in the long run where you depend on a rent roll that is artificially controlled. Rent control is a political football that does not respond to the realities of the marketplace. When fuel costs double in a single year, the politicians are very unlikely to allow more than a fraction of the cost to be passed on to tenants. The areas that have rent control laws have witnessed landlords walk away from buildings in record numbers. Rent control also makes it difficult and expensive to obtain institutional financing.

The only multiunit residential properties that are attractive in rent-controlled localities are properties too small to fall within control guidelines or those that can be converted into cooperatives or condominiums. Smaller residential rental properties include one- to four-family houses. They can produce an attractive cash flow and sometimes a nice tax-sheltered income. Larger buildings purchased for conversion are one of the hottest sectors of the housing market. The converter of a building is purchasing it at a wholesale price and selling each individual apartment at retail. Because the need for apartments remains strong in many urban areas, people will buy if they insist on a certain location and normal rentals are overpriced or unavailable.

There are, however, risks to conversion. Most readily convertible stock has already been worked upon; the popularity of conversion has raised acquisition costs to almost the same level as building new suburban condominiums; and tenant opposition may make a planned conversion impossible.

Rental houses

Renting the single-family home is a nice, safe real estate investment. There is always a large number of transferred executives seeking temporary shelter for their families in a desirable suburb. In many cases, the executive has been transferred for a fixed term, such as two years, and plans to move back home at the end of that time. Many executives keep their houses at home and rent them out in anticipation of their return. This can leave them too cash-poor for the down payment on a suitable house in the transfer city, so the employer corporation either makes a low-cost loan or subsidizes a rental. Many employers opt for rent subsidies, which put the transferred employees in the same financial position on living expenses as if they had never left home.

The rental house, as an investment, is a candidate for appreciation in almost all cases. If you find a somewhat rundown house, fix it up yourself, and rent the modernized unit to an executive, you have a chance of obtaining some extra income because the handyman special is priced below the market for comparable properties in good repair. When you buy more cheaply, the costs of mortgage service can be significantly reduced. If your monthly carrying cost is low, there may be some excess of rental income over cash outlays. This excess is probably going to be tax-free income, because depreciation, which is a noncash expense item, will shelter the excess income.

You can find tenants in various ways. You can place ads in the local paper, which a transferee is likely to obtain in his search for an appropriate rental. Or you can hire a local broker and pay a commission based on the annual rental. This varies from place to place but generally is in the range of four percent to 10 percent of the first year's rental. You might consider contacting the large companies in your area directly--send a letter to their employee division and tell them about the property you own and the rent you are asking. They may be delighted to deal with you directly if there is a shortage of desirable rental houses in your area.

You probably should not hold on to a single-family residential property indefinitely. Keep it as long as the real estate market for single-family homes in your area is rising at a rate comparable to or greater than the return you could earn on your cash in another investment. When you do sell, it will mean paying a capital gains tax on the difference between the sales price and the cost basis of the house (reduced by any depreciation taken).

Shopping centers

A small- to medium-size shopping center holds somewhere between five and 20 stores with gross rentable square footage of from 10,000 to 125,000 square feet. A roadside strip center is usually a row of three to ten stores with some available parking in the immediate area. Much of America's retail business is carried on in these centers. They usually offer basic food and service stores along with specialty stores or boutiques selling such items as antiques, jeans, and liquor.

When you consider an investment like this, it is essential to analyze the quality of all your tenants. It is ideal to have one or more solid tenants--a bank or a recognized national chain. These will attract their own clientele and push up the prosperity of all the merchants. However, be aware that there may be old, established stores with a large following in the surrounding community. They can add prestige--and shoppers--that can equal the drawing power of a national trade name.

The secret to higher rentals is a successful mix of tenants. When a lease expires, a profitable store will be prepared to pay a large rent increase, because moving might place the operation in a less successful spot. However, even if the tenant moves, a profitable location will be easy to fill with another quality tenant.

Once again, it can be worthwhile to purchase a marginal shopping center if you can upgrade the tenants. Turning a marginal shopping center into a booming one will obviously mean a larger rent roll, and that profit will directly increase the value of your investment, since real estate is most often sold on the basis of its ability to generate a specific rate of return.

Shopping centers generally represent a substantial investment. They are complicated to analyze and require a significant level of management expertise to be properly run. Because the individual investor usually cannot point to a track record of success in shopping centers, institutional lenders are often reluctant to provide backing. The individual investor, therefore, has to put up a lot of his own cash, so he cannot afford to be sloppy or inaccurate in doing his homework. The analysis must be complete and the plan of attack and operation needs to be well thought out. This is not the type of investment you should attempt in the early stages of learning about real estate.

CHAPTER THREE

Taxes and Real Estate

Would you like to hear about a good deal? Here's a description of your new business venture partner. You put up all the money and spend all the time and effort required to develop potential opportunities. If you make a profit your partner takes half or more of it. On the other hand, if you lose your shirt your losses can only be offset by your profits from other successes. The partner we are referring to is the Internal Revenue Service. In most areas of investment, this scenario is the outline of how the government works with you in your attempt to build wealth and security.

Real estate, however, is slightly different. The general tax rules governing investments contain "at risk" provisions controlling the amount of loss that can be deducted in connection with a specific investment. The "at risk" rules say that a deductible loss is limited to the amount of cash and other property the investor contributes as well as borrowed funds for which the investor is personally liable for repayment. Real property is the exception to the "at risk" rules.

In a real property investment the investor can have nonrecourse loans (on which there is no personal liability for repayment) and still take all of the tax advantages. For example, if you buy a restaurant and pay $375,000 for the business by putting up $75,000 cash and shell corporation notes for $300,000, here's what would happen if things went sour. Let's say in the first year you have a strike and the first profit and loss statement shows an operating loss of $100,000 for the year. The maximum tax deduction you can take on this investment is $75,000, since that is the amount of cash you have "at risk." The other $25,000 of loss goes into a suspense account which can only be used if the restaurant becomes profitable. Now let us say that you purchased an income property for $375,000 and put up $75,000 of cash equity and borrowed $300,000 on a nonrecourse mortgage from a bank, which took the property as security. In the first year, a major tenant goes bankrupt. Between lost rentals and fixing the space for your new tenant, the property shows a loss of $100,000. The entire loss is available to you as an offset to other income you may have. This is because in real estate an investor is not limited in loss deduction to what he has "at risk."

Let's look at another unique and interesting tax feature of real estate. When you refinance property you can take out cash in excess of your cost basis without paying tax on the money. For example, you buy a building for $100,000 and take out a $50,000 mortgage. Things go well in the real estate market and two years later the building is worth $200,000. You go to another bank and obtain a $150,000 mortgage and pay off the original $50,000 mortgage. The other $100,000 you put in your own pocket as an addition to your capital pool. No problem and no taxes. It is perfectly legitimate to take out cash in excess of your basis in the property when you refinance.

Methods of real estate depreciation

The depreciation deduction is the crux of the shelter in real estate investing. The new rules, which may be used under the Economic Recovery Act of 1981, adopt a new terminology and replace the word "depreciation" with "cost recovery." However, since the Accelerated Cost Recovery System (ACRS) for property will exist side by side with the ability to continue to claim straight-line depreciation, you will find both terms used by investors.

The net effect of depreciation is that it enables a taxpayer to keep income that would otherwise be paid to the IRS in taxes. Tax laws allow depreciation because, in theory, a building is a wasting business asset. The law assumes, apart from reality, that a building has a fixed useful life and declines in market value during that life. The owner is allowed to deduct in each taxable year the decline in value that falls into that tax year. In the real world, a well-maintained property may have a useful life that is far longer than the tax code anticipates. Thus, depreciation deductions bear little or no relationship to the actual economic decline in the value of the investment, but depreciation can often eliminate any taxable income generated by a property.

Because land is fixed and has a limitless useful life, it cannot be depreciated. Therefore, part of the purchase price should be assigned to the land and part to the improvements on the land. Obviously, the ideal is to value the building as high as possible, because it will create a high base for depreciation purposes. You should get the opinion of a professional appraiser as to the proper allocation of the purchase price between building and land. At a subsequent tax audit such an appraisal will go a long way toward establishing your case for depreciation expenses.

Under the new law, there are two kinds of depreciation on real property. They are:

1. Straight-line method. Under the straight-line method an equal amount is deducted each year for the remaining life of the property. For example, if you buy a building with a useful life of 30 years for $150,000, then straight-line depreciation is easy to calculate. Let us say that you hire an appraiser who says the land is worth $60,000 and the building on the land is worth $90,000. Under the straight-line method we could deduct $90,000 divided by 30 years which equals $3,000 each year as a depreciation expense.

2. Accelerated Cost Recovery System (ACRS). What ACRS does is put all depreciable property into one of four categories, with the cost recoverable over a 3-year, 5-year, 10-year, or 15-year period, depending on the type of property. Generally, the unadjusted basis of real property is to be recovered over a 15-year period. The IRS is to prepare a table of ACRS percentages based on the 175% declining-balance method with a switch to the straight-line method at such time as the switch will maximize the ACRS deduction. As this book goes to press, the table is not available.

The net effect of the ACRS system is to speed up the time in which a property is depreciated so that a larger deduction is available to investors each year. But it may not always be advisable for an investor to take so much depreciation shelter so quickly. Many leases provide for balloon payments in later years, and if the ACRS depreciation is taken, there would be no shelter left when substantial rental income is received. Therefore, instead of the regular ACRS deduction a taxpayer may elect to claim regular straight-line depreciation. The optional recovery periods under the straight-line ACRS election for real property are 15, 35, and 45 years. An election is made on a property-by-property basis and is revocable only with the consent of the IRS.

Depreciation not only shelters the income that might otherwise be taxable; it also converts ordinary income into capital gains when the straight-line method is used. How this works: when the property is sold, the tax laws provide for a recapture of any depreciation deductions taken while you owned the property. All depreciation deductions are subtracted from your cost basis on the property. For example, you purchased property for $110,000, of which $30,000 was allocated to the land and $80,000 to the building. Over the last five years you have taken $10,000 of depreciation deductions, which must now be recaptured on resale. The $10,000 of depreciation deduction has kept you from paying ordinary income tax (at, say, a 50 percent rate) on $10,000 of income. You sell the property for $150,000. You must pay a capital gains tax on $50,000: your cost basis of $110,000 less your depreciation taken of $10,000, subtracted from the resale price of $150,000. Capital gains tax rates are much lower than the maximum individual rate, so you save all the way around.

The new law of the accelerated cost recovery system retains the existing recapture rules for personal property and residential real property. The treatment of nonresidential real property is also unchanged if the straight-line depreciation method is used. However, for nonresidential real property depreciated under an accelerated method, gain on resale is treated as ordinary income to the extent of all prior depreciation taken by the investor.

Installment sales

You might want to attempt an installment sale of property so that your capital gains tax will fall in two tax years, perhaps because there is a possibility of your being in a lower tax bracket next year. By selling on the installment method, the recognition of gain does not occur until you actually receive payment of the purchase price, since gain is only reported to the extent that payment is actually given to you by the purchaser. So if you sell with an interest-only purchase money mortgage, you defer the gain until amortization of the principal begins.

The new rules for installment sale under the Installment Sales Revision Act passed in 1980 say that the only requirement is that payment be made in more than one taxable year. The IRS will regard all sales as installment sales unless the taxpayer makes a timely election on his tax return to report all the gain in the year in which the sale occurs. There is no longer any limit on the size of the first payment (under the old law, the seller could not receive more than 30 percent of the purchase price in the year of sale). Payment received in the year of sale is not just cash, but includes other property received and obligations of the seller that are discharged by the buyer. It also includes any amortization of a purchase money mortgage on the property received in the year of sale. For example, a seller makes a deal for $100,000 on a piece of property that we will assume has a cost basis of zero. The buyer pays $15,000 down and the seller takes back an $85,000 purchase money mortgage at 10 percent interest with monthly principal payments of $1,000. The sale takes place on March 1 with mortgage payments to begin on April 1. The buyer will pay nine months ($9,000) of principal repayment, so the seller will receive $24,000 during the first year of the installment sale ($15,000 + $9,000) of the purchase price (plus interest on the purchase money mortgage) in the first year. The seller need not elect installment sale treatment. Even if the buyer had also agreed to discharge an old $10,000 tax lien, the seller would receive installment treatment under the new law. The total purchase price received in the first year would be $34,000 but that would not prohibit installment sale election since the new law does away with the old requirement that the seller may not receive more than 30 percent of the purchase price and still elect installment treatment.

What if the seller tries to avoid having to pay the tax on yearly interest income by including interest in the installment payments and not specifying an interest rate in the contract? The consequence of such thinking is a friendly conversation with an audit agent. If the terms of sale provide for future payments and specify no interest, or a rate less than nine percent simple interest, the IRS will automatically impute a rate of 10 percent compounded semiannually. You may avoid such an imputed interest problem by specifying a nine percent simple rate. The only time the IRS won't impute interest on the unpaid portion of a sale is when no payment on the sale is due more than one year from the date of sale. Then you can increase the purchase price by one year's interest as long as the balance is fully paid in less than one year.

60 percent capital gains rule

It is a common misconception among laypeople that there is a special capital gains tax rate. When computing his tax, the taxpayer takes his total gross income, subtracts from it 60 percent of the excess net long-term capital gains over short-term capital losses, and pays taxes on the balance. The maximum individual tax rate now that the Economic Recovery Act of 1981 is in effect is 50 percent. Only 40 percent of the capital gain ends up in gross income after we subtract the 60 percent excess. Therefore, 50 percent of the 40 percent is taxed at a maximum tax rate of 20 percent.

For example, let's say you earn $50,000 of salary and in one year have a $150,000 gain on the sale of some property. Your total gross income is $200,000, a total of both types of income. In this case you may then deduct 60 percent of $150,000, or $90,000, from your gross income. This leaves you with $110,000 of income, which is subject to the maximum individual tax rate of 50 percent.

In order for you to have a capital gain or loss the thing sold must be a capital asset. If it is considered an ordinary asset then any gain or loss will be ordinary income or ordinary loss. We will examine this concept in detail below. At this point, accept the general rule that any real estate you hold for investment or use as a personal residence is a capital asset. But tuck away in your mind the thought that while you may deduct capital losses from the sale of investment property, no loss at all, capital or ordinary, may be deducted on your tax return in connection with the sale of your personal residence.

Determining the character of a gain or loss

There are four kinds of capital gains:

1. Short-term capital gains are gains on property held less than 12 months; they are taxed as ordinary income. In other words, there is no tax break.

2. Short-term capital losses are losses on property held less than 12 months, and they may be used to offset up to $3,000 per year of ordinary income with any excess of that amount carried indefinitely into the future to offset future income up to $3,000 per year.

3. Long-term capital gains are gains on capital asset property held more than 12 months; as discussed above, 60 percent may be excluded from gross income.

4. Long-term capital losses are losses on capital asset property held more than 12 months and 50 percent of such losses (a ratio of 2 to 1) may be used to offset ordinary income up to a maximum of $3,000 in any year with the balance carried over indefinitely to future years.

In any tax year the taxpayer will first offset long-term capital gains and losses against each other to arrive at a net long-term gain or loss. Next the short-term gains and losses are offset to arrive at a net short-term gain or loss. Then the tax treatment we mentioned above takes effect on the net amount of long-term or short-term gains or losses. There are many possible ways a taxpayer can end up. For example:

LTCG = Long-term capital gain

LTCL = Long-term capital loss

STCG = Short-term capital gain

STCL = Short-term capital loss

1. Mr. X has a LTCL from real estate of $50,000 and a LTCG from a stock of $10,000. He first offsets one against the other to end up with a net LTCL of $40,000. On his tax return he may deduct $3,000 in offset from his income by using up $6,000 of his LTCG (remember 2 to 1). The balance of $34,000 may be carried over to future years to offset income.

2. Mr. X has a LTCG on real estate of $50,000, a LTCL on bonds of $10,000. Mr. X has a STCL on a stock of $10,000. The two long-term items net to a LTCG of $40,000. The STCL is absorbed in the $40,000 LTCG and leaves a $30,000 LTCG.

3. Mr. X has a LTCL of $50,000 on real estate, a LTCG on stocks of $15,000. He also has a STCL of $15,000 on stocks. Thus Mr. X has a net LTCL of $35,000 and a STCL of $15,000. The STCL is used first to offset income dollar for dollar for up to $3,000. Mr. X will then carry over to next year $12,000 of STCL and $35,000 of LTCL.

4. Mr. X has a LTCG of $50,000 on real estate and a STCG of $10,000 on bonds. The STCG is ordinary income. The LTCG will be allowed the 60 percent deduction and thus have favorable tax treatment.

5. Mr. X has a LTCL of $50,000 on real estate and a STCG of $15,000 on a stock. The two are netted out and Mr. X will have a LTCL of $35,000 and can use $6,000 of it to offset $3,000 of income. The balance of $29,000 will be carried forward to future years retaining its character as a LTCL.

Remember that the ideal combination is to have a short-term capital loss and a long-term capital gain. Short-term losses can be written off dollar for dollar in income offset. Long-term gains are taxed less heavily because of the 60 percent deduction from gross income. Conversely, short-term capital gains and long-term capital losses should be avoided. Because short-term capital gains are treated as ordinary income they can be taxed at the highest individual rates. Long-term capital losses are used $2 for $1 to offset income, so a $6,000 long-term capital loss is only going to offset $3,000 of income.

Alternative minimum tax

In an effort to complicate tax laws beyond the grasp of normal mortals, 1978 brought forth legislation establishing the alternative minimum tax. It is a tax payable by an individual only if the tax amount computed under it exceeds the regular taxes plus the add-on minimum tax. So the taxpayer pays either the alternative minimum tax or the normal tax, whichever is greater. The Economic Recovery Tax Act of 1981 reduced the top alternative minimum tax rate from 25 percent to 20 percent to bring it in line with other reductions of tax rates. The tax schedule for the alternative minimum tax is a separate one. The tax rates are 10 percent on any amount between $20,000 and $60,000 and 20 percent on any amounts exceeding $60,000. Calculation of what the tax will be applied to is:

Taxable Income	+	Excluded Part (60%) of Capital Gains	+	Excess Itemized Deductions	–	$20,000 Exemption	=	Amount Taxed

The excess itemized deductions are calculated as the amount of itemized deductions (except state and local taxes, medical and casualty losses) exceeding 60 percent of adjusted gross income reduced by the same three items.

So let us say that you have $100,000 of taxable income, including the 40 percent portion of your capital gains. In addition, you have $10,000 of excess itemized deductions and $30,000 of untaxed capital gain excluded from your income under the 60 percent exclusion. We calculate our alternative minimum tax by first adding our taxable income of $100,000 to our untaxed gain of $30,000 to total $130,000. Then we add our $10,000 of excess itemized deductions and we take away the $20,000 exemption. We are left with the sum of $120,000 on which to calculate the alternative minimum tax.

Figure 3.1

Alternative Minimum Tax Calculation

10% of the amount between $20,000 and $60,000 = $ 4,000
20% of the amount over $60,000 = $12,000
TOTAL $16,000

Our alternative minimum tax liability is less than the regular tax liability on $100,000 of taxable income, so we can forget about it.

Analysis of the alternative minimum tax shows that it takes a very large amount of net long-term capital gains to make the alternative minimum tax effective. It also shows that if you have a large income, but shelter it effectively so that the regular tax rate is quite low, the alternative minimum tax is likely to be applicable (IRC Sec 55(a)(1)).

The character of a real estate gain

As we have seen from our discussions of capital gains and losses, it is important to arrange your real estate transactions to provide the right kind of income. Long-term capital gains and short-term capital losses are the most advantageous income for the investor. Poor tax planning can mean a considerable difference in the amount of profit you keep. In fact, planning is probably just as important as the investment itself. There are four characterizations of property for taxing purposes.

1. Property for Use in a Trade or Business

This is so-called "business property," and it does not matter if it is depreciable. Therefore, we may include raw land or parking lots if they are held for use in a trade or business and not for resale. If the "business property" is held for more than 12 months and sold at a profit, for tax purposes it is treated as a long-term capital gain. If the property is held for more than 12 months and sold at a loss it is an ordinary loss. This is the best of both worlds as far as tax treatment is concerned. If the property is held for less than 12 months any gain or loss is ordinary. By properly timing the sale of several pieces of business property it is possible to have the ordinary losses fall in one year to produce a tax savings and the long-term capital gain fall in another year to have favorable tax treatment. If both were done in the same year the gains and losses would have to be netted and would only serve to offset the gain.

For example, you have in your company two properties held for several years that you now wish to sell. Property X has a $50,000 loss and Property Y a $100,000 gain. If both are sold in the same year they are offset to produce a net $50,000 long-term capital gain. But if you sell Property X in year one it will be an ordinary loss and will offset $50,000 of income. Then Property Y can be sold the following year to produce a $100,000 long-term capital gain, 60 percent of which is excluded from income.

2. Investment Property

Investment property is just what the name implies. That is, property held for investment to earn a return or appreciate in value over a period of time generally longer than one year. It is one of the categories of property the conservative investor is likely to invest in. Once again, the division between long- and short-term is a 12-month holding period. Short-term gains and losses and long-term gains and losses are all capital in their treatment. Figure 3.2 compares the tax treatment of investment and business property. Note that the only category where they are alike is in long-term capital gains.

Figure 3.2

		Investment	Business
Gains	Short-term	STCG	Ordinary
	Long-term	LTCG	LTCG
Losses	Short-term	STCL	Ordinary
	Long-term	LTCL	Ordinary

3. Property held as principal residence.

As we discussed earlier, there are a great many tax advantages to owning your principal residence. In the sale of a residence held for more than 12 months, with no purchase of another residence, the gain is a long-term capital gain. But resale at a loss is not deductible.

4. Property held for sale to customers.

This so-called "dealer property" is the category which the investor wants to avoid. When property receives this type of tax treatment, all gains or losses are ordinary ones. In other words, the real property is viewed as a kind of inventory in which your regularly deal. Thus, a profit is taxed at a maximum rate of 50 percent. There is no hard and fast rule as to how the IRS determines "dealer property." They will look at the number of properties you own, the manner of acquisition, your true vocation, and the percentage of your income derived from the sales. Obviously the longer you hold a property and derive benefits from it, the more it will tend to look like an investment and will be removed from this unfavorable dealer category.

Preference taxes

In addition to regular income tax rates, there are certain preference taxes that may be imposed. They have the same objective as the alternative tax, which is to close the real estate loophole whereby ordinary income is converted to capital gains by the depreciation deduction. The item associated with real estate preference for the add-on minimum tax is the excess of any accelerated cost recovery (ACR) method over the regular straight-line cost recovery method applied over 15 years to the same property.

The add-on minimum preference tax came into being in the 1969 Tax Reform Act and was made more confused by the Reform Act of 1978, which was intended to simplify the tax code. Unlike the alternative tax, the add-on minimum tax is applied to all taxpayers, whether individuals, corporations, or partnerships.

The add-on minimum tax rate is 15 percent of the tax-preference item. A flat deduction of the greater of $10,000 or one half of your regular tax liability is taken from preference income before it is subject to the tax. The net effect of this tax on the real estate investor is that he must give back a portion of the benefits realized from the accelerated cost recovery shelter each year. Still, it is not too bad a deal. Consider that you have had use of the government's money during the years; this tax is a repayment of the loan. In order to fall into the preference tax category, you need to have a significant amount of accelerated cost recovery system deduction or have a low taxable income.

Tax-free methods

There are three tax-free methods of disposing of real estate: involuntary conversions, sale of a residence, and exchanges of like-kind investment and trade property. We have already dealt with the favorable provisions of the tax law as it pertains to a residence. We shall concentrate here on involuntary conversions and like-kind exchanges.

If a taxpayer loses his property through no choice of his own, a tax-free exchange may take place. Such involuntary conversion occurs when the property is destroyed in a calamity (fire, earthquake, tornado, flood), or is condemned or threatened with condemnation by federal or local governments. A new road, an addition to a school, government office requirements, or other condemnation for the public good may leave you with one less real property holding. Compensation from an insurance company for a calamity loss or from a government for a condemnation loss has no immediate tax consequences if it is invested in similar property. But if what you buy as a replacement costs less than what was received, the excess is taxed. You are allowed three years from the condemnation of real property to find something else to buy; in casualty conversion the time is reduced to two years.

By far the most common tax-free method of disposing of real estate is the like-kind exchange. "Like-kind" does not mean that the properties must be identical. Improved real estate, like an apartment house, can be exchanged for raw land, provided both properties were held for investment purposes or trade or business purposes. The exchange may include cash or other additional payment, called "boot," to equalize the value of the exchange. By continuing to exchange, the seller can defer paying taxes and reinvest the full amount of capital in new properties. In effect, the IRS is giving the taxpayer an interest-free loan. Be aware, however, that a tax-free exchange applies to profits and losses alike, so if you have a loss and make an exchange, the loss will not be recognized.

It is not uncommon to find a three- or four-party like-kind exchange. For example, A has a property that B wants to buy. A will not sell outright but will swap it with B if he will buy the properties owned by C and D and include them in the exchange. B must first buy the two properties and then swap them with A for the property he wishes to own. One caveat: never try to short-circuit the whole mess by having C and D transfer their properties directly to A. For the possible savings of an extra transfer tax you may lose the tax-free status of the transfer.

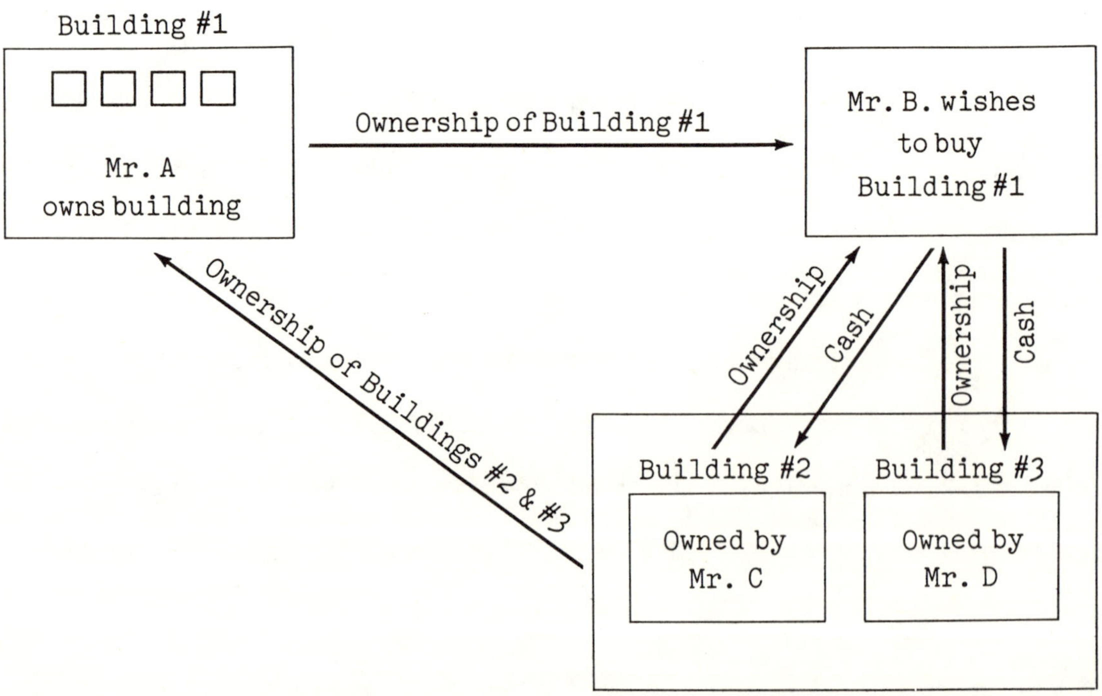

1. Mr. B wishes to buy Building #1 owned by Mr. A.

2. Mr. A will not sell outright because of tax on his appreciated value but will swap Building #1 for Buildings #2 and #3.

3. Mr. B buys Building #2 and Building #3 from their owners and pays the transfer tax. He now owns Buildings #2 and #3.

4. Mr. B swaps Buildings #2 and #3 with Mr. A for Building #1.

You may swap real estate for a lease interest and still have a like-kind tax-free transaction. As long as the lease is for more than 30 years it is treated as an interest in real property.

Let's look at the case of Mr. A who owns an apartment building worth $2,500,000 in which he has an equity of $1,600,000. There is an assignable mortgage on the building of $900,000. Mr. B has a shopping center worth $3,000,000 in which he has a $2,000,000 equity and a $1,000,000 mortgage. Mr. A and Mr. B want to exchange properties. There is an equity difference of $400,000 between Mr. A's apartment building and Mr. B's shopping center. Mr. A will have to pay "boot" of $400,000, which can consist of cash, notes, property, or anything that Mr. A and Mr. B can agree upon. For simplicity we shall say that lower and higher rate mortgages have been taken into account and the mortgage figures above are net after premiums or discounts.

First, net out the mortgages. Mr. A was relieved of a $900,000 mortgage and Mr. B of a $1,000,000 mortgage. Mr. B was relieved of a net $100,000 of mortgage and this gets added onto his $400,000 "boot" for tax purposes to make it total $500,000. (Note that if B had a $2,000,000 mortgage he would not make the swap because he would have a $1,500,000 "boot"!)

If the value of the qualified property transferred plus the boot received is greater than the calculated basis in the property transferred, a gain is recognized but not in excess of the boot.

We apply the following formula:

Old Basis in the Property Swapped

1. Increased by basis in the boot
2. Decreased by any money received; and
3. Increased by any gain; and
4. Decreased by loss on boot; and
5. Increased by additional mortgage liabilities; equals

Basis in new property

Don't panic, as this is not really very difficult; it is purely mechanical. In our example let us say that Mr. A will pay the $400,000 difference in the "boot" by giving Mr. B stock he bought for $500,000 which is now worth $400,000. Here is the result of our formula:

	For Mr. A	For Mr. B
Old basis in property swapped	$600,000	$1,500,000
1. Plus basis in "boot"	500,000	-0-
2. Minus money received	-0-	(400,000)
3. Plus gain on transaction	-0-	500,000
4. Minus loss on "boot"	(100,000)	-0-
5. Plus additional mortgage liabilities	100,000	-0-
Basis in new property	$1,100,000	$1,600,000

Mr. A will recognize his $100,000 loss on the stock part of his "boot." He will take over the shopping center with a $1,100,000 basis. Mr. B will take over the apartment house with a $1,600,000 basis. Mr. B will have to pay a tax on the amount of his gain realized up to the fair market value of the "boot." Mr. B paid $1,500,000 for the shopping center and swapped it for $3,000,000 so he has a gain of $1,500,000. This gain will be recognized up to the value of the "boot" (or $500,000). Don't worry if you can't immediately repeat all of this formula. Your accountant will do the actual work. Just be aware that in these swaps there are changes in basis and potential taxes in the "boot."

Selling subject to a mortgage

It's not unusual to find a qualified buyer for your property who, for one reason or another, cannot obtain a mortgage. You may still wish to dispose of the property, so you check with your banker, who says you should assign the outstanding mortgage to the purchaser. For example, you bought a building for $500,000 in 1976. At the time of purchase you put up $100,000 of cash equity and obtained a $400,000 mortgage. The building has been held for five years and depreciated on a straight-line basis. In all, you have taken $200,000 of depreciation, and as we discussed earlier, this means that your adjusted basis is $300,000 (purchase price less depreciation). The mortgage has been paid down in its principal amount so that $350,000 of the $400,000 originally borrowed is still outstanding.

If the property is sold for $600,000 to a purchaser who assumes the $350,000 balance on the mortgage, here is your position.

Proceeds of sale	$600,000
Minus mortgage balance	350,000
Cash to seller	$250,000

Your capital gains tax will be figured on the difference between the $600,000 purchase price and your $300,000 adjusted basis. This will yield a net long-term capital gain of $300,000 that may cost you $60,000 in capital gains tax, so the net amount realized will be $190,000. But what if you have to give the purchaser a second mortgage for $250,000? Will you still owe the $60,000 tax even though you received no cash at the closing? Yes, you will have to pay the capital gains tax in any event.

Let us change this scenario just slightly, in another example. What if you buy the same $500,000 building with $100,000 of equity and a $400,000 mortgage? Oil costs shoot up, the area changes for the worse and rents have to be lowered, and the cash flow can't carry the building. You go to your bank and say that the building has turned sour. You don't want it and the bank can take it back. The banker mulls this over and says that he can change the present principal balance due on the mortgage from $350,000 to $250,000. The added cash flow makes everything profitable again, so you agree. Note that the cancellation of indebtedness income is taxable to you! However, you may avoid recognizing the gain by reducing the basis of the property. In this example, the $100,000 of forgiven mortgage would reduce your basis to $400,000.

Estate and gift taxes

If you can't take it with you then you aren't going! Right? Wrong, as far as anyone knows. Since you might want to hedge your bets a little, some family tax-planning is in order. The Economic Recovery Tax Act (ERTA) of 1981 provides for an increase in the unified credit against estate and gift taxes from the 1981 figure of $47,000 to $192,800. This rise will take place gradually from 1982-1987 and will have the effect of raising the size of an estate passing free from estate and gift taxes from the 1981 level of $175,000 to a 1987 level of $600,000. The phased-in increases go as follows:

YEAR	CREDIT	"EXEMPTION EQUIVALENT"
1982	$ 62,800	$225,000
1983	79,300	275,000
1984	96,300	325,000
1985	121,800	400,000
1986	155,800	500,000
1987 and later	192,800	600,000

The Tax Reform Act of 1976 provided an estate tax marital deduction equal to the greater of $250,000 or one-half of the adjusted gross estate for property passing to a decedent's spouse. The new ERTA of 1981 eliminates the monetary ceiling on the estate (and gift tax) marital deductions for people dying after 1981. So, if you can hang on until 1982, then unlimited amounts of property can be transferred between spouses free of estate or gift taxes.

There is still a valuable estate loophole that is significant in very large estates. The accelerated cost recovery (depreciation) in a piece of real estate avoids tax on the death of an individual because it is given to an heir at a tax basis equal to the fair market value of the property as of the date of the death of the donor. This is called the stepped-up basis of an asset. For example, Mr. X buys property for $750,000 and over a period of 10 years takes ACRS deductions of $500,000 so that his basis in the property is $250,000. On his death the property passes to Mr. X's son, and the son's basis will be calculated as $900,000--the fair market value on the date of Mr. X's death. The estate of Mr. X will pay estate tax on the fair market value of $900,000. By dying and passing the property in his will Mr. X and his heirs avoided all recapture of ACRS deductions used through the last 10 years.

CHAPTER FOUR

Shopping for Property

For reasons that are difficult to understand, the world is full of people who would rather save a commission dollar than earn three dollars. These people will go to any length to avoid paying a brokerage commission. Any length often means overpaying for property or else being unaware of all of the possibilities for investment. So let's make it clear that, by and large, most brokers are trained and experienced salespeople. Their fee is based on a percentage of the sales price the buyer pays for property the broker has shown. Broker commissions vary, but they generally range from five percent to seven percent of the sales price.

The contract almost always says that the seller pays the brokerage commission. That is what it says, but you can be sure that isn't the whole truth. A seller who agrees to a six percent brokerage fee and wants to walk away with $100,000 for his property will put it on the market for $110,000.

He figures that will give him $3,400 of price flexibility and still pay for the $6,600 brokerage commission. The net result is that the buyer actually absorbs the cost of the brokerage fee in his purchase price even though the seller hands the broker a check at the closing.

The buyer should never look upon the broker as a partner or an ally. Under the present system, in theory, the broker is really employed by the seller. What this means is that you should not discuss purchasing strategy with him or her. All planning should be done out of earshot of both the seller and the broker. It also means that not everything said about the buyers competing for the property is likely to be entirely true. As you gain experience you will hear some of these common ploys:

"There's a lot of action on that property and many brokers have shown it."

"Put your bid in now so you'll have priority."

"Many people in our office feel the price is much too low."

"Better buy before the spring (substitute summer, fall, winter as appropriate) market heats up."

"I know they won't take anything less than the asking price."

"The seller is thinking about raising the price because of the activity."

If this type of maneuvering bothers you, let someone else (such as your lawyer or accountant) do your negotiating. Little white lies promote action and thought and aren't taken too seriously by experienced negotiators.

What you ought to take seriously is the basic factual information the broker supplies about the property. As we will see later, there are many financial computations to be made before the purchase of any property. The result of this work is only as good as the data used in calculating the results. A good broker will tell you about the quality of his information. If it comes from financial statements prepared by an accountant, you should ask for a copy. On the other hand, if it is an oral estimate from the seller given to the broker over the phone, you have a right to ask specifics about the source of the numbers.

Let us also remember the phrase caveat emptor. The buyer should beware of the seller and deal on an arms-length business basis. If you forget to ask about the cost of heating a building, don't expect the broker to volunteer the amount. A broker is not going to share in either your profit or loss on a property. He is only going to supply those facts and figures that you have the good sense to ask for. As long as what is supplied is true to the best of the broker's knowledge, he has done his job. It's up to you to do a thorough job in your homework.

Approaching a broker

Brokers are not mind readers. Before you visit or telephone one, you must have some idea about the kind of real estate investment that would be attractive to you. You can decide this after you work through your own finances, read this book, and speak with friends who have made several real estate investments. If you have a regular lawyer or accountant, it may also pay to discuss the concept with them. Then sit down and carefully fill in the information in the following broker's worksheet. It is probable that the first time you fill out this worksheet your return on investment and return on cash figures will be unrealistically high compared to what is available in the market place.

The number of brokers you should approach depends on the type of property you are buying and the location you want. In urban areas, it is best to have a network of broker contacts. This is fairly easy to establish by using the local newspaper's real estate section. The really active brokers may even specify which area of the city is their specialty. For example, in New York City, it is common to see "Specialists in the West Side" or "East Side is our specialty." If you are interested in a particular urban area, use the specialist along with other general brokers for the widest possible selection of opportunities.

In rural areas meeting and dealing with brokers is slightly different. There is generally not a wide selection of brokers, and it is quite common to find one-person organizations. Not all the property that is for sale is even listed with a broker. Because of the small town flavor of the business, some potential sellers may have only had a conversation with the broker about their property, with a ballpark price that would make the seller willing to entertain an offer. Perhaps the actual listing was not finalized because the seller did not want to be the focus of local gossip. So it helps to be as specific as possible about the kind of property you want when you're dealing with rural brokers. Then solicit their opinion as to prices in the area and have them substantiate it with some recent transactions. Their sales figures can and should be verified at the county clerk's office or wherever deeds and property tax records are kept.

In recent years there has developed a new type of broker who is part of a regional or national broker chain. The idea is to be able to give organized coverage of potential opportunities in a wider market. These firms have tended to specialize in residential housing because they can cater to relocated executives. They can sell or rent the house in one location and also obtain the sale or rental of the new residence. If you are thinking of investing in nonowner occupied single-family houses and renting them, the national chains are probably good sources of potential investments as well as tenants.

Some words about best using a professional broker's services are in order here. A good broker is your screen on the marketplace. He should take you to see properties of potential interest to you and not waste your time by showing things that are way out of your price range, unrelated to your interest area, or not priced near the market. This means that some excellent brokers only call certain clients once or twice a year. They have done the necessary screening and you should give serious attention to their opinion. On the other hand, a broker who calls every day with a new deal that he says is sensational is probably so anxious to sell you something--anything--that you will accomplish nothing. The best thing to do is back off gently and find a new broker. If that is not possible in a certain locality, try to sit down with the broker and firmly reinforce your investment guidelines and objectives.

Industrial and commercial properties have fewer brokers with larger territories. This is probably because the nature of commercial transactions is much more complicated and requires greater skill to execute. Some industrial and commercial properties are listed for sale by their owners in the real estate section of local papers. They are also listed in national financial papers such as the Wall Street Journal. However, if you use a commercial broker you must be prepared to evaluate a property promptly.

BROKER'S WORKSHEET

Cash available for investment $____________________

Approximate net worth $____________________

Approximate tax bracket __________%

Objective of Investment (check and number in importance)

Tax shelter	__________
Income	__________
Capital appreciation	__________
Diversification	__________
Other	__________

Minimum Acceptable Returns

Return on cash	__________%
Return on investment	__________%

Individual Experience

		Yes	No
Familiar with management of:			
	Land	____	____
	Apartment buildings	____	____
	Commercial property	____	____
	Shopping centers	____	____
	Industrial property	____	____
	Rental houses	____	____
Knowledge of renovation		____	____
Familiar with construction		____	____
Financial background		____	____
Legal background		____	____

Previous lease negotiation ______ ______

Comfortable with high leverage ______ ______

Geographic Preference for Property

Local ____________________

County ____________________

Statewide ____________________

Other ____________________

Tenant Preference

Individuals ____________________

Stores ____________________

Small business ____________________

Large business ____________________

Other ____________________

Other comments: ____

____

____

____

Information Wanted from Broker

Local maps

Local history

List of area banks

Schedule of commission charges

Financial statements on property

There are many prospective buyers for desirable properties, and speedy decisions to enter serious negotiations with the seller are important.

When you go out with a broker to review a property, bring along a pad and pencil. It is not possible to retain all of the details necessary for making a firm decision to buy or pass by. You might consider keeping a file for each broker with a sheet on each property shown. This will tell you how well the broker is working on your behalf, what the marketplace looks like, and build your own file of comparable records. It even pays to inquire later about the actual selling price of a property you did not buy. This can serve as a check on your estimates of value and your skill at real estate investment decisions.

Selecting a lawyer and accountant

An old myth about lawyers and accountants is that the "A" students teach, the "B" students suffer, and the "C" students endow the university. The tax law and accounting regulations in general, and for real estate in particular, have gotten very complex. Seek out the scholarly "A" students, because you need the best advice obtainable. You need good advice every step of the way because tax implications can be more important than the gross profit on the deal. Losses, of course, need to be taken in the most advantageous way possible in light of your own tax position. A good real estate lawyer or accountant works in the field continuously and is up to date with recent developments.

Your best source of finding a good adviser is through word of mouth. Ask around and you will probably get several recommendations. Then consider the source of the referral in terms of sophistication, personal success, and experience in real estate investments. You don't need the highest priced real estate lawyer at a large New York law firm to buy a single-family house. Conversely, don't expect a local accountant who has dealt in rural real estate to give you proper advice on the purchase of an urban office tower. No matter how good and conscientious a professional may be, it puts a strain on his abilities when he is asked to work in an unfamiliar area.

Interviewing a prospective lawyer or accountant will do both of you some good. From your point of view you will get some information about the way he operates. Be sure to ask up front about professional fees and charges. Get a rate for aid in negotiations, research, drawing papers, and closing a deal. Also find out if he will work with you on a failed transaction at a lower than normal rate. Most professionals charge more for successful deals, since everyone makes money, and lower their fees when the charges are straight overhead. Don't forget to lay out your long-term plan for building up real estate assets. If you appear to be a long-term client, a lawyer or accountant can become an important personal adviser. Their experience will be invaluable.

There is no clear-cut answer as to when you need both a lawyer and an accountant. When the time comes you will know it. In general, the lawyer is your best first step. A lawyer who truly understands real estate investing will also be well versed in the accounting aspects of the field. He may be the one who suggests that you employ a good accountant to help keep your investment strategy in line with your other personal affairs.

If you can't locate a lawyer through a recommendation, there are several other methods. First, get information on any real estate seminars in your area. The chances are that several lawyers will be speakers. This is your chance to learn something about the field as well as to meet and listen to several potential advisers without incurring initial visit charges. If you don't like that method, ask either the account officer at your local bank or the local bar association to make some recommendations. Of course, the further afield you go in your search for an adviser, the more careful you must be to conduct a thorough interview.

Professional inspectors and appraisers

On the investment level of purchasing a single-family house for rental purposes, a professional inspection means very little. A house is generally what it appears to be, since the method of construction and the local building code assure some consistency. Listed in the yellow pages are many inspectors who will come and give you a three or four page check-off inspection for $50 to $200. If you are a neophyte and know absolutely nothing about heating, plumbing, or general repairs, this may be useful. It provides a slight measure of comfort--with no guarantee the house won't collapse tomorrow.

Buying a larger rental property is a different ball game. The division of purchase price between building and land will determine how much depreciation you will be able to take. A professional appraisal, done long before any audit, will support your position on how you allocated the purchase price. For example, you buy a building and land for $100,000. The local assessment of $30,000 for property taxes breaks down to $20,000 (or two-thirds) for the building and $10,000 (or one-third) for the land. According to the assessment you can allocate $66,000 of the purchase price to the building and then begin depreciation. If you have a professional appraiser certify that 80 percent (or four-fifths) of the purchase price should be allocated to the building and 20 percent (or one-fifth) to the land, you are much better off. You may depreciate from an $80,000 base as opposed to a $66,000 base. If you should be questioned in an audit, the professional appraisal will go a long way toward substantiating the higher base.

In very large real estate transactions a professional inspector with an engineering background and a reputable appraiser are necessities. You should not presume that your own technical background can replace a detailed opinion on quality of construction. Such inspections or appraisals are expensive, and fees vary according to the size and nature of the transaction. The best full-time real estate speculators regularly use inspectors and appraisers for major property investments, and you should do the same. Locate such people through your broker, accountant, professional trade associations, or the real estate department of a large commercial bank or insurance company. See Chapter Nine for further information on inspection and appraisal.

CHAPTER FIVE

Raw Land

Buying unimproved raw land because it's not being made any more is foolish. As we said earlier, the key element in land investment is location. When someone buys your land he is buying a location for a purpose. The land itself just happens to be a space that is not yet fulfilling that purpose.

More than two-thirds of the land in the United States is rough and undeveloped, so raw land is not a scarce commodity. The scarcity is in the spot shortages in particular areas made desirable by their location within a unique regional development.

As we enter the age of energy problems, locations in developed areas will have even greater potential for appreciation than in the past. The suburban sprawl generated by the artificially low gasoline prices of the last two decades is likely to cease. No longer will large developers be building giant office and shopping complexes at great distances from population centers. The cost of fuel, and its availability, will be major factors in the individual's decision to shop or work in remote locations. Even recreation centers will have to adjust to the fact that distance will become an obstacle in attracting vacationers. An inaccessible mountain in the far reaches of Vermont will have fewer skiers than before, regardless of its natural beauty.

Having given some of the negative aspects of raw land, it is appropriate to focus here on the positive attributes of this kind of investment. Properly chosen raw land has the best potential return of any real estate investment. Raw acreage in a natural state has the ability to multiply two, four, even ten-fold in value if it turns out to be the most desirable location for growth in a particular area. For example, a potentially well located suburb of a city has an area within it with an inherent physical defect. The raw land has poor drainage and is something of a swamp. During the early years of development in the suburb, homes will be constructed on the surrounding plainland since it is the easiest to develop. The swamp property has few buyers and is priced well below the other land. At some point in time, however, it will pay to drain the swamp and utilize the location. Indeed, it may turn out to be the last large chunk of space in an affluent suburb. This would make it highly desirable for more residential housing or for a multitude of commercial uses.

Raw land has the highest leverage value on pure space. What this means is that raw land is low-cost space when compared to any form of developed income-producing property. So the play in raw land is that an investor has acquired space that can either be further developed by the investor or sold to another for development. The space is being purchased at its lowest level of use and the investor speculates that a higher level of use will become desirable in the future. To grasp the concept of the highest probable level of use, compare a wild mountain area to the skyline of huge buildings on Manhattan island in New York. Only a very small fraction of land will ever become so desirable that builders will cover it with as many skyscrapers as Manhattan has.

Analysis of a raw land investment is not easy and is not entirely scientific. There is no exact calculation which will give the investor a picture of the future development pattern which will emerge. However, the positive and negative factors of raw land speculation are set out in Figure 5.1.

Figure 5.1

Raw Land Investment

Advantages	Disadvantages
1. Highest leverage on raw space.	1. Highest risk real estate investment.
2. Relatively low cost investment.	2. No income is produced while it is being held.
3. Potential gain is much greater than on developed properties.	3. Financing is difficult, and in some cases impossible to obtain.
4. Requires little attention and management.	4. Hidden physical defects can wipe out the investment.
	5. Local regulation may inhibit the best use of the property.

Looking for raw land

It is not very likely that you will get a truly great buy on raw land through a broker. Speculation in land requires being on the scene before it is apparent to everybody that the area has the potential for significant growth. That means there are not many buyers. In such circumstances, no broker would be able to make a living. The speculator in raw land, using our conservative investment philosophy, will find himself dealing directly with farmers, local lenders, estates, and government authorities. Of these, farmers and estates are usually your best bet for a fairly uncomplicated sale.

The basic tool for investigating raw land is a map. Maps of all kinds are readily available from sources such as major oil companies, the U.S. government, local chambers of commerce, and even tourist bureaus. Road maps are important because they can give you a good idea of the accessibility of an area to the neighboring community. Land that is situated along major routes has value just because people can get to it. Street maps allow you to pinpoint the availability of services in relation to a particular piece of land. If you are speculating on residential growth make notations on an overall master map about:

1. Commutation to urban working centers.
2. Shopping areas.
3. Fire stations.
4. Availability of electric power.
5. Schools.

Lastly, there are topographical maps (called "topo" maps) on just about every area of the United States. These maps show the physical attributes of the area in great detail. They earmark every natural phenomenon, including height of each area, type of terrain, unusual features, and natural boundaries. The United States Geological Survey (USGS) prepared these maps, and they are available at most sporting goods or hiking stores.

If you can't find what you want, write to the National Cartographic Information Center, 507 National Center, Reston, Virginia 22092.

In approaching a raw land investment try to obtain a feel for the history of the area. This does not mean touring Indian campgrounds and the sites of colonial settlements. World War II, around 1945, is usually a good starting point. You should follow the development of population growth in the surrounding areas. The expansion of industry and transportation will often be key elements. People move and live where jobs are available. Retail business tends to follow people, since population creates the demand for goods and services. Once there is an established labor pool with particular skills, more industry will be attracted. Then the process begins to feed on itself as business, suburbs, and retail development all grow together.

In any given area, try to pinpoint new road and rail construction. It is a pretty safe bet that the next thrust of growth will follow transportation. The very early stages of highways are often not widely publicized. They may exist in the concepts of a local planning board, state agency, or even federal agency. You can obtain information on such development in a particular area from local builders, planning boards, housing departments, building inspectors, congressmen, the mayor, and a host of other sources. Draw in such potential development on your local maps. Then comes the hard part. You will have to make some kind of value judgment about the likelihood of such plans going forward in the near future. Timing is quite crucial. Having the foresight to buy land 100 years in advance of improvements will obviously not produce an immediate investment profit.

If you have investigated an area and are convinced that it is a sound investment, the next step is locating land to buy. If you do it without a broker, you'll need to use some creativity. Putting an ad in the local paper for "land wanted" is a nice, straightforward approach. It often produces results and the technique may be part of your repertoire. There are more aggressive methods that might also work. Old fashioned legwork is one. Go around to talk to the present owners of property that you feel might be particularly desirable. You may very well put the idea to sell in their heads by discussing the matter. Just be sure you've done your homework and know the relative value of raw land and farmland in the area. A ridiculously low offer will attract few takers.

One side note is important here. Don't drive up to a farmer in a $50,000 sports car. Likewise, don't wear designer clothes, gold watches and chains, and handmade shoes. Try to talk to the man on a level to which he can relate. Your first physical impression will be very important in establishing that rapport. Also, attempt to listen more than speak. If he is a third generation farmer on that land, to whom he sells the land may be almost as important as the price he receives. The present owner wants to like the buyer. Needless to say, your plan to knock down his house, dig up the orchard, and fill in the pond to make room for parking cars are all details that should be omitted from the conversation.

If you know you lack the initiative and creativity for this kind of self-lead generation, it is still possible to deal in raw land. There are, in some areas, country brokers who sell raw land. The likelihood of getting a truly great buy will be gone, but there is still an opportunity to hold the land for its next best use. Most of the same map and history homework is still in order. With a broker, however, there may be records of other comparable sales in recent times to assure you that you have not overpaid. The commission you pay the broker may well be worth it if he can generate reasonably good potential leads priced somewhere near their value.

Inspection

Physical inspection of raw land is a necessity before you buy. Even with a topographic map it is impossible to grasp the full potential of property sight unseen. If you believe the future of your raw land lies in residential housing, try to get a feel for:

1. Views.
2. Type of small foliage currently on the land.
3. Location and age of trees.
4. Amount of rock outcrops.
5. How well the land will drain.

It never hurts to call in professional engineers, surveyors, and the like in a raw land speculation. So much can go wrong that it is almost impossible for the layman to cover all the bases. For example, in an area where there will be no sewer hookup, waste disposal is done through septic tanks. These disperse the waste through an area of ground called the septic field. If the quality of the soil itself will inhibit such waste disposal you may have a real problem building houses on the land. At the very least, the density of units will be reduced and this will affect profitability.

Water on a piece of land is usually a positive feature. But if you see a wide stream bed and a narrow stream, look out. The property might well be right in the path of spring runoff from melting snows. This can turn a darling little brook into a roaring swell of water that can flood the entire property at certain times. Finding out about flooding is crucial. This can be done through insurance companies and state or local flood control authorities.

Access to utilities is another thing to be concerned with during your physical inspection. Call up the local power company and ask about their hookup charges. Find out if the developer must pay for running new lines throughout the property. This might be a significant expense. Also, if you are thinking of residential projects, inquire as to whether you need to run sewer lines, drains, and curbing. Items like these can make it impossible to use the land profitably, because the selling price of houses would have to be above the average market price in the area.

Formulating a bid

Before you can decide what to pay you must make a guess about how long you intend to hold the property. This will enable you to calculate carrying costs and what you will want to resell the property for in the future. Earlier we used a time line to show the present or future value of an investment. In the chapter on financing techniques there will be a mathematical focus on time value calculations. At this stage, just rough out the details. For example, a 25 acre raw land investment requires a cash purchase price of $50,000. You expect the new highway to reach your land in, at most, five years. Taxes are fairly constant at $1,100 per year. If you want a return of 12 percent or more on your capital, the minimum sales price you need to obtain in five years is about $96,500. That works out to a price of about $3,850 per acre for raw land. In the developed areas served by the highway at the time of purchase, the price of $3,850 should be close to the going market rate. If it is lower than the local price per acre, then you will probably do that much better when you eventually resell.

If the price being asked appears much too high in light of the amount of money you must tie up and the time you expect for turnaround resale, something must give way. Either the purchase price must come down or the amount of cash must be substantially reduced. The seller may stick to a particular selling price, but you can reduce the actual cost of holding the land by stretching the length of time needed for the premium payout. For example, what if our 25 acres at $50,000 turn out to be overpriced at $3,850 per acre. Perhaps the seller might be satisfied with $20,000 in cash, interest only for five years at eight percent, and the balance of $30,000 due at the end of the fifth year.

Figure 5.2

	$20,000	$1,100 2,400	$1,100 2,400	$1,100 2,400	$1,100 2,400	$30,000 2,400 1,100
Yr.	0	1	2	3	4	5

Then our total cost looks quite different at the end of five years. It would look like the total in Figure 5.2.

5-year future value $20,000 @ 12%	$36,334
Total taxes	5,500
Total interest	12,000
Final payment	30,000
	$83,835

This is quite a bit lower than the all-cash offer and brings the price per acre down to about $3,350.

We could also allow the seller to take a very low amount of cash on the front end, guarantee a minimum of $50,000 at the end of five years, and give the seller a share of the profits from resale above the $50,000 price. So let us say we bid $5,000 cash down, interest only for five years at eight percent, the balance of $45,000 due at the end of the fifth year, and 25 percent of the net profits from resale over $50,000. Why would the seller accept this arrangement? Perhaps the $1,100 per year of taxes on the land are a burden. Instead, the seller would be receiving a positive interest income of $3,600 that he may apply to other purposes. In addition, if the land skyrockets in value the seller will share a healthy part of the good fortune. In the reverse situation, he has a minimum of $50,000 that will be realized from his asset.

Always evaluate raw land in terms of the way in which you intend to resell it. If you are going to sell the entire package off at one time, that is quite different from a price based on a number of subdivision plots. The smaller the units you sell, the higher their price. For example, if you buy land that can be used for 25 buildable housing lots for $50,000, you have paid $2,000 per lot. Individual lots may well be retailed for $3,000 to $6,000 each, depending on location. However, you will have to wait much longer to make 25 sales than to make one wholesale transaction for the entire piece. Thus you will want the seller to extend longer-term financing to induce you to purchase the property.

The point of our discussion here is that institutional financing for raw land is virtually nonexistent, so you have to look to the seller to make the deal work. Whatever the original terms proposed by the seller, they have to be altered if they don't fit economic reality. If you can't live with what the seller asks, counter with something that makes sense to you as the purchaser. The absolute worst that can happen is that the seller will say no. Then again he may propose a compromise that suits both of you. If he is adamant, look for another investment. It's better to walk away and seek a new opportunity than to overpay or be stuck with the wrong kind of financing.

Options

When speculating in raw land, one of the most valuable tools the purchaser can use is an option. We may define an option as a contractual right to purchase specific property at or before some specified point of time (the expiration date) in the future. An option may be exclusive or nonexclusive. If it is exclusive, the purchaser is the only potential buyer at a price that is fixed in the option. If it is a nonexclusive option the seller may have reserved the right to have other potential purchasers bid along with the option purchaser, who has the right of first refusal to match the highest outside bid. If the option purchaser does not match the highest outside bid on the property, then the seller is free to accept the offer of the other purchaser. If the option purchaser matches the highest bid, the seller is bound to transfer the property to him.

Until an option is exercised by the purchaser, the seller retains full ownership of the property. Exclusive options allow a great deal of leverage to the buyer. If the price of the land rises quickly the option purchaser has locked in a bargain purchase price for a low fraction of the overall increased value of the property. Once priced, the buyer of the option risks only the amount paid for it. An option can be allowed to expire without any execution and the buyer has no further obligation.

There are many conditions that can be made part of the option contract to induce the seller to enter into an option agreement. Some of the more common are:

1. The purchaser of the option agrees to help pay for carrying costs of the land (such as taxes or mortgage).

2. The purchaser agrees to allow the seller to participate in profits made in subsequent resale.

3. The purchaser of the option agrees to pay an increased purchase price equated to the length of time the seller keeps the property off the market.

On the other side of the coin, the seller who grants the option may allow the purchaser some of the following rights:

1. The purchaser has an option to buy all the property but can buy smaller portions at various times. This allows the purchaser to test for the potential success of development. If things don't work out the purchaser need not make the total commitment.

2. The price of the option can be credited to the eventual selling price.

When an option is exercised the purchaser must give notice of his intention to use his rights prior to the expiration date. The option will almost always specify that the notice must be in writing, delivered to the seller at a certain address, so many days before the expiration date.

Managing raw land investments

We said earlier that raw land requires little time when compared to other real estate investments. There are, however, certain basic things that need to be done. The property should be kept in good condition and not allowed to be overgrown with weeds and brush. A fence may prevent others from using the land as a dumping ground. Of course, the cost and likelihood of this problem should be weighed before undertaking any protective measures.

You might be creative and have others defray the carrying costs and sometimes even enhance the value of your land. For example, if there is a deep gully that would need filling for any future development, consider soliciting clean fill. Allow builders in the area to dump unwanted soil or rocks in the designated spot to help fill the depression. There are even some possibilities for creating income from a piece of raw land.

1. Sharecropping is a good possibility if you are buying farmable acreage. You allow a farmer to grow crops on your land. In return, as owner, you are entitled to a percentage of the profits realized when the crops are sold. Of course, this is a somewhat risky business because crops are vulnerable to weather and market conditions and so will not guarantee an income.

2. A fixed rent ground lease to a farmer is a better bet since it assures income for the year. However, many farmers shy away from such fixed overhead.

3. Recreational campgrounds or trailer parks can be very profitable if run correctly. They require management, as does any business.

4. Advertising billboards, where they are permitted, are an excellent source of income with relatively few management problems.

5. Use of natural resources such as water, grass for grazing, timbercutting, and the like are other potential uses of land.

Zoning

The days of total freedom in using your property are gone forever, replaced by the concept of zoning for permissible uses. Zoning can control whether the land can be commercially or residentially developed, how many units per acre can be built, parking requirements, height requirements, style of architecture, setbacks from the road, curb cuts for driveways, and almost any other element that a local politician can conceive of. In many areas there is an unpaid zoning board that reviews the plans of all potential developers. They are often powerful, inconsistent, petty, and frustrating. If you aren't a local citizen the cards may be stacked against you.

Changes in zoning can significantly increase or decrease the value of property. They can move land up to a higher commercial use with its attendant increase in income. Therefore, it is common for the purchaser to set the price of a raw land purchase contingent on certain zoning. Success in changing zoning means the transaction moves forward as planned, and failure can reduce the purchase price or even terminate the deal.

Before you even consider buying land in a particular area, check out any zoning problems. Ask around to find out if the zoning board has a reputation for being very tough on new development. You can ask local builders, brokers, and even landowners. Most zoning board meetings are a matter of public record. Ask someone whose name appears in a recent matter what he thinks of the local situation. If things look very bad, weigh that as a cost of the purchase. You may have to shoulder a long lawsuit against the zoning board before being able to develop your land. But if you win, the increase in value may well be worth the risk.

Checklist for raw land

Desirable characteristics

1. Attractive foliage.
2. Relatively uniform terrain.
3. Available water supply.
4. Access to good roads.
5. Utilities available nearby.
6. Growing population in the surrounding areas.

Undesirable characteristics

1. Swamp or marsh areas.
2. Land not accessible to the main road.
3. Lack of industry in surrounding area.
4. Large rock outcrops.
5. Temperamental zoning board.

Resale

1. Estimated resale time.
2. Taxes.
3. Interest and other carrying costs.
4. Management of the property.
5. Offsetting income available.

Potential use

1. Residential
   - i) Single-family homes.
   - ii) Multi-unit residential.
2. Commercial.
3. Industrial.

CHAPTER SIX

Purchasing Problem Properties

There are many reasons why a particular piece of real estate can suddenly become unprofitable. Sometimes the financing is set at the prime rate plus certain points, a basis that was appropriate at the time it was arranged. A sudden surge in borrowing rates pushes up interest costs to the point where they produce a serious cash drain. In other cases, the surrounding economy can be thrown into a crisis by a deep recession or the closing of a major business employer. Rental income can drop dramatically and force the property below a break-even level of operation. Of course, there is also the possibility of a natural calamity such as a flood, tornado, or the like that disrupts or permanently alters the local economy. While the property in question may not directly suffer the consequence of the calamity it may indeed have an adverse effect on the area. For example, a standard joke after the accident at the Three Mile Island nuclear power plant was that local residents could save on electricity because their real estate glowed in the dark. It may seem funny to an outsider, but owners of surrounding real estate lost the ability to attract tenants or to dispose of their property at anything close to pre-accident prices.

In looking at problem properties, it is most important to weigh the point of view of three parties. These parties are the seller, the new investor, and the underlying mortgage lender. All three must cooperate in the effort to rehabilitate the property. The seller may indeed be faced with a loss of some magnitude. However, he must be convinced that the real issue is not how much he will lose, but rather how much he can salvage. The new investor must be aware that most of the potential for success will come out of the losses of the other two parties. Finally, the lender must take a reasonable position to avoid having to foreclose and operate the property itself.

In the following sections of this chapter we shall consider some of the more common problems in real estate and propose what to do about them. As a practical matter, the proposed solutions will not work in all cases because there will be unique circumstances that cannot be covered in this book. However, some experience will go a long way toward enabling the investor to cure a problem parcel with some minor adjustments to the techniques described.

Overfinanced property

We have already seen that leverage has two facets. It dramatically increases profits on invested capital in a good investment, but it can also accelerate decline in a calamity. The single most common cause of financing problems is a floating loan that is pegged to the prime rate or some other recognized indicator. With the wide fluctuations in money markets that have occurred in recent years, interest carrying costs have been known to double in a single year. Since this is a major component of operating expense, the net result has been that many buildings were thrown, almost overnight, into a negative cash flow position. This has a dramatic effect on the value of a property and its liquidity. The pool of available investors willing and able to obtain financing that will return a positive cash flow is small. Certainly, the added risk will be reflected in a much lower sales price.

The first course of action in overfinanced properties is to meet with the lenders. A mortgagee may consider a reduction in interest rate if the problem has not been caused by inept management or substantial payments to a junior lender. For example, a building is purchased for $1,000,000 with 20 year bank financing of $600,000 at the rate of prime plus two. The former owner also extended a $300,000 self-liquidating purchase money mortgage at a fixed rate of 18 percent for a term of eight years. At the time of initial financing, the prime rate was eight percent. Some years later the prime rate has risen to 19 percent and the building becomes a problem property with a negative cash flow. The bank, as senior lender, may insist that the junior lender (the former owner) do one or more things before it will reduce its steep interest charges of 21 percent. First, the bank may insist that the term of the purchase money mortgage be extended to a longer time period to reduce amortization. It may even put a large part of the loan into a balloon payment. Second, the bank could insist on a reduction in the interest rate on the junior lending portion which matches or exceeds its own concessions.

A senior lender has a considerable amount of authority and control in the case of problem property. The senior lender may commence foreclosure actions that if carried out, might wipe out the junior lender's entire position. Just the threat of foreclosure is a very effective method of forcing concessions that will redirect a problem property into a positive cash flow position. Most institutional lenders are reasonable in their demands and use the power of the senior lender in an appropriate manner. But keep in mind your inferior position as a junior lender if you decide to sell an investment and take the bulk of your profit in a purchase-money mortgage.

A related solution to extending the term or lowering the interest rate on a purchase-money mortgage is buying it out completely. The loan, due to the problems of payment and its subordination to other financing, will be sold at a substantial discount. That means that it will not be worth the $300,000 face amount in our example but might well sell as low as 30 to 50 percent of this amount. If the purchase-money mortgage represents only profits of the previous owner, the senior lender is apt to be more hardnosed and offer a lower buyout price. If the junior loan comes from a second mortgage company, the senior lender is less likely to push for a removal of the second mortgage at a deep discount.

Neglected property

Buildings are frequently allowed to deteriorate and become less desirable in the marketplace. Sometimes this happens because an owner has done very well on his investment and no longer feels any urgency to be aggressive. The tenants have been there for many years, the value of the building has tripled over its initial purchase price, and the owner has received back his equity investment many times over in cash flow and depreciation benefits. Physical upkeep reverts to minimal efforts to repair problems as they occur, and the overall quality of the exterior appearance declines. The fundamentals of the building, its location, and its profitability are not permanently altered by such developments.

An investor who locates this kind of property can obtain a jewel in the rough at a discount price. An infusion of capital for repairs will probably be needed, but it can be followed by better tenants and a healthier rent roll. If you have a good track record, a lender may even include the cost of repairs in the amount of permanent financing extended. Without doubt, this type of conservative real estate investment can bring your portfolio of properties along very nicely--just don't expect to find it on a regular basis.

Overtaxed property

Real estate taxes are often the second largest component of expenses on property behind interest and amortization of financing. It is not unusual, when property changes hands, to have the local assessor pay a visit. A significant increase in taxes might be justified by the assessor on the basis of the fair market value transaction price as compared to the assessed value. This is especially true if the previous owner held the property for a long time, and the area did not have any physical reassessments. The previous owner may have only had tax increases computed on the basis of rising tax rates for the whole area as opposed to the actual increase in value of his income property.

If you come across property that might be profitable with a change in tax rates, you may be able to obtain a reduction. It will be necessary to demonstrate to local authorities the adverse impact of excessive taxing by revealing income and expense items in some detail. The municipality has much to gain in keeping a building from deteriorating because there is no positive cash flow to support repairs. Preservation of the quality of the neighborhood can be a powerful negotiating position.

A senior institutional lender can aid in your dealings with the local authorities. The local government will want to encourage the institution to extend credit in the form of mortgages in their community. Two kinds of relief are usually sought. First, you may want a temporary tax abatement while repairs are being made. Then, this may or may not be coupled with a permanent reduction of the assessed value. If you can obtain a list of comparable values and rent rolls from buildings in the area and relate them to the amount of taxes paid, this may also be helpful. The amount of taxes on any property is a matter of public record that you can research at the assessor's office. The size of rent rolls, on the other hand, is more difficult to find out. Brokers can help and some owners may be encouraged to reveal such numbers if the lender also holds their mortgage.

Construction lending distress

The construction loan is almost always at a rate which floats above the prime rate. Quick changes in the credit environment can have dramatic cash draining impact and create a problem construction project. The lenders may then insist that the developer put up more security or find an investor who can do so.

In addition to financing problems, there are a host of other unknowns affecting real estate construction. Labor strife, failure of a subcontractor to perform, environmental problems and the like can endanger continuation of the project. In New York City, a developer put up a large residential highrise and completed all work on the building except the bathrooms. His supplier of toilet bowls went bankrupt and no other manufacturer could supply the quantity needed on short notice because there was a construction boom and output was already fully contracted. That project literally went into the tank.

Investing in projects that have had difficulty in the construction loan phase and sought new investors for completion is risky. You must first make the judgment that the completed project will be viable and profitable. Then you must be sure that your investment will carry things over the top and allow eventual completion. This is not the kind of investment which should be chosen by a passive and inexperienced real estate investor. Speak to the construction lender when weighing the risks and find out its view of the project and its construction schedule. Don't forget to inquire whether the inspections made under the construction loan revealed shoddy workmanship or the use of inferior grades of materials.

Foreclosure

In some circumstances an owner and his lenders (and other creditors) cannot come to agreement on a workout plan. Then the mortgagee begins the legal process of foreclosing on the mortgage because of the borrower's default. In most mortgages there is an acceleration clause allowing the mortgagee to make the whole loan due and payable if one or more payments are not timely made. When a loan is accelerated, the mortgagor can either pay off the loan in full or have his rights to the property pass to the lender. The lender then sells the property and uses the proceeds to satisfy any outstanding mortgage debts. If there is an excess, it is returned to the owner of the property.

If a mortgage is foreclosed and no third party bids a reasonable price that will satisfy the mortgage debt, the lender will usually buy the property. The mortgagee has a bad debt deduction equal to the difference between the mortgage owed it and the price it paid. In addition the mortgagee has a gain or loss to the extent the price paid exceeds or is less than fair market value. If there are no third party bidders, the mortgagee will make a low bid and get a large bad-debt deduction. The lender as the only bidder can then claim that its bid is the fair market value unless the IRS can prove to the contrary. Ergo, the lender has no capital gain because it did not buy below fair market value.

The former owner of the property sold at foreclosure also has some tax problems. Although not personally liable for the mortgage debt, the owner will have a cash capital gain tax expenditure for any amount by which the loan forgiveness exceeds his adjusted basis. For example, if you own a building with a $350,000 mortgage, and an adjusted basis of $250,000, let us consider what may happen upon foreclosure. The bank will cancel $350,000 of indebtedness and take the building to sell it and satisfy the mortgage. You will have a $350,000 cancellation of indebtedness versus a $250,000 adjusted basis, which will produce $100,000 of capital gains. Note that in this situation if the bank did not take the building in foreclosure but instead forgave $100,000 of the mortgage outright, you still would have that $100,000 as capital gains. However, under present IRS regulation you can avoid recognizing this income by reducing your basis in the property by the amount of forgiven debt (to $150,000).

Let us consider another case, where some real estate turns sour, the property is foreclosed, and the owner suffers a loss. Suppose he bought a property for $250,000 and put up $50,000 in cash and borrowed $200,000 from a bank. Over a period of years the mortgage has been amortized by $25,000 and depreciation of $30,000 has been taken. Suddenly, and for various reasons, the property is in trouble; after much negotiation the lenders foreclose and sell it for $175,000, which pays off the full mortgage balance. The original basis of the property is $250,000 less $30,000 depreciation, yielding an adjusted basis of $220,000. The net cash proceeds from foreclosure are $175,000, so the owner will have a loss of $45,000 subject to the capital loss provisions.

Bankrupt tenants

Sometimes a good property becomes a problem because of the unexpected bankruptcy of a principal tenant. A good example of this occurred when W.T. Grant filed for bankruptcy and left many landlords around the country with large vacant stores and a significant loss of rental income. The first place to turn in such circumstances is to the lenders for a moratorium on payments. An owner may also seek a new investor with the capital to change the space to meet the needs of new tenants. This kind of investment can frequently prove very rewarding. Good locations are never plentiful, so it is quite likely that new tenants can be secured at a better rent and on better terms.

Government controls

If a property has developed a negative cash flow because of rent control or some other regulatory cap on rental income, it's probably a poor investment. The inhibitions on the free market rental rate imposed by social considerations are likely to be impossible to remove. Most experienced real estate investors know that trying to reason with entrenched government programs is time-consuming and doomed to failure. Only a reconsideration of local tax assessment, as we said earlier, is a good bet. The conclusion is that you should avoid buying property in areas where rent control regulations are in force. An artificial market is using investors' capital to underwrite a social program of low-cost housing. You are not likely to realize any appreciation on your investment.

Real estate workouts

Let's face it, any legal proceeding is an expensive and time-consuming problem for an institutional lender. Foreclosure has a particularly bad ring and lenders want to avoid it whenever possible. Therefore, the real estate workout can present opportunities for the investor. The term "workout" is applied to the process by which lenders, developers, and creditors devise a plan for completing a real estate project that has run so far over budget that it cannot be completed with the cost structure by which it was originally undertaken. Sometimes it is just a matter of changing the financing arrangements and strengthening the creditworthiness of the project. In other situations it may mean a total rework of concept, design, and execution of the project. In either case, planning a workout is difficult. Here are some basic steps you should take in considering a workout in investment.

1. Construct an accurate financial picture of the operating costs of the project at this point in time. The numbers should be as completely detailed as possible. An accountant familiar with the essentials of real estate would be a valuable asset.

2. Analyze the proposed or completed project to see if its size and scope are appropriate. You don't want to buy into grandiose plans that just don't fit the community.

3. If it's a construction workout, look into the reputation and experience of the builder and developer. A long track record of success is an excellent recommendation. Even the best builder or developer can have difficulties on a project due to unforeseen circumstances.

4. Consider the lender in the project and that lender's experience in this kind of real estate loan. Local banks do not generally understand development construction as well as insurance companies. They may be placing unreasonable demands on the developer that a more sophisticated lender might not request. On the other hand, local banks may know more about the local market values than a distant institution and thus be correct in insisting on more equity and less leverage.

5. Work out a financial pro forma schedule of the cash flow for workout. This should be a full rundown on how things should go from the present to a profitable future. (See the forms provided at the end of this chapter.)

6. Set out the details of the senior lender's position on interest charges, amortization, and potential equity in the property, and where it might end up.

7. Draft a plan for junior lenders, recognizing that they will be in

the worst position and might be touchy.

8. Investigate sources of new funds that might be available. These may be institutional or governmental.

9. Break down the various tasks involved in the management of the property and find out what could be improved. If it is an established building or development, assess the job to date and make all the necessary changes in staff or overhead.

10. Look at the tenant mix to judge if it is a good one. In a commercial property in trouble, it is sometimes possible to obtain capital from tenants who want to maintain the location.

11. Secure all of the previously executed documents such as mortgages, bonds, letters of credit, and extensions.

12. Try to insulate yourself from the past problems by a corporate policy of strictly limited liability.

13. Attempt to settle any present lawsuits to the satisfaction of the parties without litigating.

14. Understand all of the legal and tax ramifications involved in the workout. Once again, this is where an experienced real estate lawyer is a necessity.

15. Try out your solution on one party at a time on an informal basis.

A workout plan assumes that you have the financial and real estate expertise to solve other people's problems. Everyone who made the initial investment thought they knew all of the essential elements. Obviously they were wrong. Therefore, make a judgment about how much of the failure could have been avoided by better planning, and recognize what risk elements were beyond everyone's control.

A sample workout

In the following pro formas you can see how a professional planner formats the financial details of an attempted workout of an office building. This building will be called 8 Thomas St., and it represents an actual problem real estate investment located in Massachusetts. The property is a three-story office structure built over three levels of parking for 576 cars, on two and three-quarters acres of land. In all, the building has 171,123 gross square feet of space with 151,518 net rentable square feet, with 3.4 parking spaces allocated to each 1,000 square feet leased by each tenant.

Because of labor difficulties and increases in the cost of supplies, the initial loan for the complex was completely used up on January 1, 1980. This loan was for 100 percent of the projected cost. It was made by a commercial bank for a total amount of $8,300,000. At the time the building ran into difficulties, it was projected that the additional amount required to achieve a pro forma workout in 1981 was $342,327. The bank determined that the overall projected return on the total of initial loan and additional funds would be set at 14.6 percent. As the building rents up, the pro forma cash flow from operations, before debt service, is projected at $1,265,953 per year.

The bank has taken over ownership and now wishes to recover its funds. Our pro formas are structured to rent up the entire building by June of 1981. The bank is attempting to determine what market price the project could be sold for and when the most opportune time would be to sell. The building is 72 percent occupied as of January 1, 1980, and the base building is 100 percent completed.

PROJECTED PRO FORMA 1981
8 Thomas St., Inc.

171,123 gross rental square feet
151,518 net rental square feet

INCOME		
Rental (net)		
Leased	127,475 sq. ft. @ $ 9.38	$1,195,716
Unleased management space	2,304 sq. ft. @ $13.00	29,952
Unleased construction space	558 sq. ft. @ $13.00	7,254
Unleased space	32,861 sq. ft. @ $13.00	427,193
Additional space-N.E. Telephone	2,109 sq. ft. @ $12.50	26,362
Pending lease	5,816 sq. ft. @ $13.00	75,608
	171,123 sq. ft.	$1,762,085
Roll-over for 1980		
Mass. Teachers	$ 13,452	
Best Food	5,268	
Polaroid Corp.	47,940	
N.E. Telephone	56,349	123,009
TOTAL RENTAL		$1,885,094
ELECTRICITY: (1)		
TAX ESCALATION:		45,136
OPERATIONAL ESCALATION:		51,374
PARKING:		1
OVERTIME CHARGES:		1
		$1,981,606
Less: 5% vacancies		(99,080)
Effective gross income		$1,882,525
EXPENSES:		
Payroll, taxes & benefits	$ 44,000	
Repairs & maintenance	16,000	
Contract services (including cleaning)	89,000	
Utilities (net) (1)	117,000	
Administrative	61,000	
Insurance	34,000	
Management space	29,000	
Replacements	12,000	
Operating expenses, excluding real estate taxes ($2.35 sq. ft.)	$402,000	
Real estate taxes ($1.26 sq. ft.)	$214,910	
TOTAL OPERATING EXPENSES ($3.61 sq. ft.)		616,910
Cash flow from operations before debt service		$1,265,616

(1) Electricity: Basic charge		
Leased	127,475 @ $ .42	$ 53,540
Unleased	43,648 @ $ .60	26,188
Net against utility expense		$ 79,728

PROJECTED INVESTMENT AT PRO FORMA 1981

8 Thomas St., Inc.

			BUDGET
INVESTMENT TO DATE (January 1, 1980)			$8,300,000
Additional funds required			
Construction			
Base building	$100,000		
Tenant improvements @ $11.06 53,459 sq. ft.	591,257		
General repairs	10,000		
Total additional construction		$701,257	
Leasing commissions, advertising and marketing		195,495	
Legal, accounting, general and administrative		65,000	
Contingencies		75,000	
(LESS:) Cash flow from operations		(694,425)	
Additional funds required			342,327
TOTAL PROJECTED INVESTMENT AT PRO FORMA 1981			$8,642,327

Per square foot gross $50.50 sq. ft. Net $57.04 sq. ft.

GENERAL REPAIRS
MARCH, 1980

	BUDGET	ACTUAL PAID TO DATE	BALANCE TO FUND	% COMPLETE
General repairs	$10,000	--	$10,000	--%

LEASING COMMISSION, ADVERTISING AND MARKETING
MARCH, 1980

	BUDGET	ACTUAL PAID TO DATE	BALANCE TO FUND	VARIANCE
Leasing commissions (Peter Allan & Co.)	$130,495	$ 8,625	$121,870	
Advertising	65,000	4,690	60,310	
TOTAL	$195,495	$13,315	$182,180	

102

CASH FLOW FROM OPERATIONS DURING RENT-UP

8 Thomas St. Inc.

	1980 BUDGET	1981 BUDGET
INCOME:		
Rental (net)	$1,272,173	$1,718,111
Electricity (netted below)	--	--
Real Estate Tax Escalation	45,124	50,310
Operating Expenses Escalation	39,392	44,906
Effective Gross Income	1,356,689	1,813,327
EXPENSES:		
Payroll, Taxes, & Benefits	45,688	52,084
Repair & Maintenance	18,850	21,490
Contract Services (Inc. Cleaning)	100,755	114,860
Utilities--Net	127,029	139,820
Administrative	78,990	106,330
Insurance	34,000	38,760
Management Space	29,952	29,952
Replacements	12,000	13,680
Operating Expenses, excluding Estate Taxes	447,264	516,976
Real Estate Taxes	215,000	232,200
Total Operating Expenses	662,264	749,176
Cash Flow From Operations	$ 694,425	$1,064,151

LEGAL, ACCOUNTING, GENERAL AND ADMINISTRATIVE

MARCH, 1980

	BUDGET	ACTUAL PAID TO DATE	BALANCE TO FUND	VARIANCE
Legal	$20,000	--	$20,000	
Accounting	30,000	--	30,000	
General and Administrative	15,000	--	15,000	
TOTAL	$65,000		$65,000	

INCOME AND CASH FLOW STATEMENT

8 Thomas St., Inc.

	FOR THE MONTH OF MARCH, 1980			
	ACTUAL	% TO RENT AVAILABLE	BUDGET	VARIANCE
Rent Available	$149,860	100.0%	$149,860	$ -
Less: Vacancies	(49,994)	(33.4)	(49,994)	-
Management Space	(604)	(.4)	(604)	-
Allowances[1]	150	.1	-	150
Net Rental	99,412	66.3	99,262	150
Other Income:				
Operations	12,072	8.1	3,958	8,114
Other	-	-	-	-
Total Income	111,484	74.4	103,220	8.264
Operating Expenses:				
Payroll	3,266	2.2	3,808	542
Repair & Maintenance	1,106	.7	1,571	465
Contract Services	7,202	4.8	8,394	1,192
Utilities	14,920	10.0	10,586	(4,334)
Administrative	9,065	6.0	12,633	3,568
Real Estate Taxes	18,376	12.3	17,917	(459)
Total Operating Expenses	53,935	36.0	54,909	974
Net Income Before Depreciation & Amortization	57,549	38.4	48,311	9,238
Adjustment to Cash Flow	(5,180)	(3.5)	(86,396)	81,216
Cash Flow	$52,369	34.9%	$(38,085)	$90,454

[1] Net of Accounts Receivable collected for prior months and this month's Accounts Receivable.

FOR THE THREE MONTHS ENDED MARCH 31, 1980

ACTUAL	% TO RENT AVAILABLE	BUDGET	VARIANCE
$444,642	100.0%	$444,642	$ -
(153,368)	(34.5)	(153,368)	-
(1,812)	(.4)	(1,812)	-
(9,766)	(2.2)	-	(9,766)
279,696	62.9	289,462	(9,766)
35,682	8.0	26,539	9,143
14	-	-	14
315,392	70.9	316,001	(609)
10,662	2.4	11,424	762
3,521	.8	4,713	1,192
26,897	6.0	25,182	(1,715)
16,773	3.8	31,758	14,985
26,050	5.9	38,237	12,187
55,128	12.4	53,751	(1,377)
139,031	31.3	165,065	26,034
176,361	39.6	150,936	25,425
(16,665)	(3.7)	(259,188)	242,523
$159,696	35.9%	$(108,252)	$267,948

OPERATING EXPENSES

8 Thomas St., Inc.

	FOR THE MONTH OF MARCH, 1980			
	ACTUAL	% TO RENT AVAILABLE	BUDGET	VARIANCE
OPERATING EXPENSES				
PAYROLL:				
Maintenance	$ 2,154		$ 2,301	$ 147
Administrative	740		815	75
Payroll Taxes	336		317	(19)
Employee Benefits	36		375	339
Total Payroll	3,266	2.2%	3,808	542
REPAIR & MAINTENANCE				
Windows	-		62	62
Air Conditioning	352		85	(267)
Heating	-		125	125
Electrical	-		-	-
Building Supplies	290		450	160
Lighting	164		100	(64)
Locks/Key Replacement	-		40	40
Carpentry	-		-	-
Supplies	18		100	82
Plumbing	202		75	(127)
Roof	-		167	167
Deck/Waterproofing	-		167	167
Miscellaneous	80		200	120
Total Repair & Maintenance	1,106	.7%	1,571	465
CONTRACT SERVICES				
Security	2,180		2,383	203
Rubbish Removal	432		433	1
Snow Removal	-		83	83
Window Cleaning	-		83	83
Cleaning	3,482		4,200	718
Landscaping	-		62	62
Elevator	509		495	(14)
H.V.A.C.	570		625	55
Exterminator	29		30	1
Total Contract Services	7,202	4.8%	8,394	1,192
UTILITIES				
Water	137		157	20
Gas	-		17	17
Electric	14,783		10,412	(4,371)
Steam	-		-	-
Sewer	-		-	-
Total Utilities	14,920	10.0%	10,586	(4,334)

FOR THE THREE MONTHS ENDED MARCH 31, 1980			
ACTUAL	% TO RENT AVAILABLE	BUDGET	VARIANCE
$7,044		$6,903	$(141)
2,405		2,445	40
1,099		951	(148)
114		1,125	1,011
10,662	2.4%	11,424	762
-		186	186
469		255	(214)
-		375	375
537		-	(537)
918		1,350	432
164		300	136
114		120	6
77		-	(77)
110		300	190
202		225	23
-		501	501
850		501	(349)
80		600	520
3,521	.8%	4,713	1,192
7,310		7,149	(161)
1,178		1,299	121
183		249	66
-		249	249
13,830		12,600	(1,230)
-		186	186
1,527		1,485	(42)
2,782		1,875	(907)
87		90	3
26,897	6.0%	25,182	(1,715)
511		471	(40)
77		51	(26)
16,185		31,236	15,051
-		-	-
-		-	-
16,773	3.8%	31,758	14,985

OPERATING EXPENSES

8 Thomas St., Inc.

	FOR THE MONTH OF MARCH, 1980			
	ACTUAL	% TO RENT AVAILABLE	BUDGET	VARIANCE
ADMINISTRATIVE				
Legal	$ -		$ 292	$ 292
Accounting	693		417	(276)
Telephone	32		100	68
Consulting	150		75	(75)
Supplies	-		100	100
Management Fee	6,014		5,220	(794)
Miscellaneous	93		100	7
Insurance	2,083		2,833	750
Management Space	-		2,496	2,496
Replacements	-		1,000	1,000
Total Administrative	9,065	6.0%	12,633	3,568
REAL ESTATE TAXES	18,376	12.3%	17,917	(459)
TOTAL OPERATING EXPENSES	$53,935	36.0%	$54,909	$ 974

FOR THE THREE MONTHS ENDED MARCH 31, 1980

ACTUAL	% TO RENT AVAILABLE	BUDGET	VARIANCE
$ -		$ 876	$ 876
693		1,251	558
432		300	(132)
450		225	(225)
-		300	300
17,968		15,998	(1,970)
258		300	42
6,249		8,499	2,250
-		7,488	7,488
-		3,000	3,000
26,050	5.9%	38,237	12,187
55,128	12.4%	53,751	(1,377)
$139,031	31.3%	$165,065	$26,034

RENT-UP SCHEDULE

8 Thomas St. Inc.

JANUARY 1, 1980 TO DECEMBER 31, 1981

TOTAL	171,123 sq. ft.
RENTED	127,475 sq. ft.
BALANCE TO RENT	43,648 sq. ft.
LEASE EXPIRATION Jan. 1980 - Dec. 1981	75,916 sq. ft.
BUDGETED TO RENT	119,564 sq. ft.

	SQUARE FEET				AVERAGE $13 PER SQ FT.			
	BUDGET	ACTUAL	MONTHLY VARIANCE	VARIANCE YEAR TO DATE	BUDGET	ACTUAL	MONTHLY VARIANCE	VARIANCE YEAR TO DATE
1980								
Jan.	701	701	-	-	$ 9,113	$ 6,660	$ 2,453	$ 2,453
Feb.	-	-	-	-	-	-	-	2,453
March	5,709	2,918(a)	2,728	2,728	74,217	41,257	32,960	35,413
April	8,883				115,479			
May	3,899				50,687			
June	2,728				35,464			
July	4,446				57,798			
Aug.	2,728				35,464			
Sept.	2,728				35,464			
Oct.	39,043				507,559			
Nov.	2,728				35,464			
Dec.	14,443				187,759			
Total	88,036				$1,144,468			
1981								
Jan.	2,728				$ 35,464			
Feb.	2,728				35,464			
March	2,728				35,464			
April	2,728				35,464			
May	3,446				44,798			
June	7,559				98,267			
July	-				-			
Aug.	1,366				17,758			
Sept.	-				-			
Oct.	584				7,592			
Nov.	4,013				52,169			
Dec.	3,648				47,424			
	31,528				$409,864			

(a) Ax Grind Assoc. are tenants-at-will with new monthly rent of $13.84 per sq. ft., or $3,438.09 per month.

CASH FLOW COMPARISON

JANUARY 1, 1980 THROUGH DECEMBER 31, 1980

8 Thomas St., Inc.

	OPERATIONS			RENT-UP AND BALANCE OF CONSTRUCTION			TOTAL			
1980	BUDGET	ACTUAL	VARIANCE	BUDGET	ACTUAL	VARIANCE	BUDGET	ACTUAL	VARIANCE	CUM. VARIANCE
Jan.	$ 50,776	$51,858	$ 1,082	$ (86,396)	$(10,565)	$75,831	$ (35,620)	$41,293	$ 76,913	$ 76,913
Feb.	51,849	66,954	15,105	(86,396)	(920)	85,476	(34,547)	66,034	100,581	177,494
Mar.	48,311	57,549	9,238	(86,396)	(5,180)	81,216	(38,085)	52,369	90,454	267,948
Apr.	49,983			(86,396)			(36,413)			
May	51,279			(86,396)			(35,117)			
June	56,851			(86,396)			(27,545)			
July	58,352			(86,396)			(28,044)			
Aug.	70,699			(86,396)			(15,697)			
Sept.	63,172			(86,396)			(23,224)			
Oct.	62,529			(86,396)			(23,867)			
Nov.	62,529			(86,396)			(23,867)			
Dec.	68,095			(86,396)			(18,301)			
TOTAL	$694,425			$(1,036,752)			$(340,327)			

(1) Operational cash flow has a positive variance of $9,238 as a result of increased escalation income.

(2) Rent-up and construction cash flow is under budget as a result of a timing difference.

CASH FLOW BUDGET
Jan. 1, 1980 Through Dec. 31, 1980

	JANUARY	FEBRUARY	MARCH	APRIL	MAY
INCOME					
Gross Possible	$147,391	$147,391	$149,860	$152,311	$152,382
Less: Construction Office	(604)	(604)	(604)	(604)	(604)
Less: Vacancies	(51,687)	(51,687)	(49,994)	(49,994)	(48,697)
Net Rental Income	95,100	95,100	99,262	101,713	103,081
Real Estate Taxes Escalation	7,445	8,574	677	--	--
Operating Expenses Escalation	3,281	3,281	3,281	3,281	3,281
Electricity (Net against expense)	--	--	--	--	--
Parking Fees	--	--	--	--	--
TOTAL INCOME	105,826	106,955	103,220	104,994	106,362
OPERATING EXPENSES:					
PAYROLL	3,808	3,808	3,808	3,808	3,808
REPAIR AND MAINTENANCE	1,571	1,571	1,571	1,571	1,571
CONTRACT SERVICES	8,394	8,394	8,394	8,394	8,394
UTILITIES:					
Water	157	157	157	157	157
Gas	17	17	17	17	17
Electricity - Net	10,412	10,412	10,412	10,412	10,412
Steam	--	--	--	--	--
Sewer	--	--	--	--	--
TOTAL UTILITIES	10,586	10,586	10,586	10,586	10,586
ADMINISTRATIVE					
Legal	292	292	292	292	292
Accounting	417	417	417	417	417
Telephone	100	100	100	100	100
Consulting	75	75	75	75	75
Supplies	100	100	100	100	100
Management Fee	5,361	5,417	5,220	5,322	5,394
Miscellaneous	100	100	100	100	100
Insurance	2,833	2,833	2,833	2,833	2,833
Management Space	2,496	2,496	2,496	2,496	2,496
Replacements	1,000	1,000	1,000	1,000	1,000
TOTAL ADMINISTRATIVE	12,774	12,830	12,633	12,735	12,807
REAL ESTATE TAXES	17,917	17,917	17,917	17,917	17,917
TOTAL OPERATING EXPENSES	55,050	55,106	54,909	55,011	55,083
CASH FLOW FROM OPERATIONS	50,776	51,849	48,311	49,983	51,279
ADJUSTMENT TO CASH FLOW	(86,396)	(86,396)	(86,396)	(86,396)	(86,396)
NET CASH FLOW FROM OPERATIONS	$(35,620)	$(34,547)	$(38,085)	$(36,413)	$(35,117)

JUNE	JULY	AUGUST	SEPTEMBER	OCTOBER	NOVEMBER	DECEMBER	TOTAL
$152,382	$152,382	$152,838	$152,838	$152,838	$152,838	$152,838	$1,818,289
(604)	(604)	(604)	(604)	(604)	(604)	(604)	(7,248)
(48,697)	(48,697)	(37,883)	(37,883)	(37,883)	(37,883)	(37,883)	(538,868)
103,081	103,081	114,351	114,351	114,351	114,351	114,351	1,272,173
5,866	7,445	8,574	677	--	--	5,866	45,124
3,281	3,281	3,285	3,285	3,285	3,285	3,285	39,392
--	--	--	--	--	--	--	--
--	--	--	--	--	--	--	--
112,228	113,807	126,210	118,313	117,636	117,636	123,502	1,356,689
3,808	3,808	3,808	3,808	3,808	3,808	3,808	45,688
1,571	1,571	1,571	1,571	1,571	1,571	1,569	18,850
8,394	8,394	8,394	8,394	8,394	8,394	8,421	100,755
157	157	157	157	157	157	157	1,884
17	17	17	17	17	17	13	200
10,412	10,412	10,412	10,412	10,412	10,412	10,413	124,945
--	--	--	--	--	--	--	--
--	--	--	--	--	--	--	--
10,586	10,586	10,586	10,586	10,586	10,586	10,583	127,029
292	292	292	292	292	292	288	3,500
417	417	417	417	417	417	413	5,000
100	100	100	100	100	100	100	1,200
75	75	75	75	75	75	75	900
100	100	100	100	100	100	100	1,200
5,688	5,766	5,822	5,452	5,418	5,418	5,712	65,990
100	100	100	100	100	100	100	1,200
2,833	2,833	2,833	2,833	2,833	2,833	2,837	34,000
2,496	2,496	2,496	2,496	2,496	2,496	2,496	29,952
1,000	1,000	1,000	1,000	1,000	1,000	1,000	12,000
13,101	13,179	13,235	12,865	12,831	12,831	13,121	154,942
17,917	17,917	17,917	17,917	17,917	17,917	17,913	215,000
55,377	55,455	55,511	55,141	55,107	55,107	55,407	662,264
56,851	58,352	70,699	63,172	62,529	62,529	68,095	694,425
(86,396)	(86,396)	(86,396)	(86,396)	(86,396)	(86,396)	(86,396)	(1,036,752)
$(29,454)	$(28,044)	$(15,697)	$(23,224)	$(23,867)	$(23,867)	$(18,301)	$(342,327)

CASH FLOW BUDGET*
Jan. 1, 1981 Through Dec. 31, 1981

	JANUARY	FEBRUARY	MARCH	APRIL	MAY
INCOME:					
Gross Possible	$157,447	$157,447	$157,447	$157,447	$157,447
Less: Vacancies	(31,212)	(26,824)	(22,437)	(18,049)	(13,661)
Less: Construction Office	(604)	(604)	(604)	(604)	(604)
Net Rental Income	125,631	130,019	134,406	138,794	143,182
Real Estate Taxes	8,040	9,260	730	--	--
Operating Expenses	3,742	3,742	3,742	3,742	3,742
Electricity	--	--	--	--	--
Parking Fees	--	--	--	--	--
TOTAL INCOME	137,413	143,021	138,878	142,536	146,924
OPERATING EXPENSES:					
PAYROLL					
Maintenance	2,623	2,623	2,623	2,623	2,623
Administrative	928	928	928	928	928
Payroll Taxes	360	360	360	360	360
Employee Benefits	427	427	427	427	427
TOTAL PAYROLL	4,338	4,338	4,338	4,338	4,338
REPAIRS AND MAINTENANCE:					
Windows	71	71	71	71	71
Air Conditioning	96	96	96	96	96
Heating	--	--	--	--	--
Electrical	142	142	142	142	142
Building Supplies	513	513	513	513	513
Lighting	114	114	114	114	114
Locks/Key Replacement	45	45	45	45	45
Carpentry	--	--	--	--	--
Supplies	114	114	114	114	114
Plumbing	85	85	85	85	85
Roof	190	190	190	190	190
Deck/Waterproofing	190	190	190	190	190
Miscellaneous	228	228	228	228	228
TOTAL REPAIRS AND MAINTENANCE	1,788	1788	1788	1,788	1,788

*Continued on page 116.

JUNE	JULY	AUGUST	SEPTEMBER	OCTOBER	NOVEMBER	DECEMBER	TOTAL
$157,716	$159,081	$159,081	$159,423	$159,423	$159,569	$160,901	$1,902,429
(9,269)	(9,269)	(9,269)	(9,270)	(9,270)	(9,270)	(9,270)	(177,070)
(604)	(604)	(604)	(604)	(604)	(604)	(604)	(7,248)
147,843	149,208	149,208	149,549	149,549	149,695	151,027	1,718,111
6,335	8,040	9,260	730	--	--	7,915	50,310
3,742	3,742	3,742	3,742	3,742	3,742	3,744	44,906
--	--	--	--	--	--	--	--
--	--	--	--	--	--	--	--
157,920	160,990	162,210	154,021	153,291	153,437	162,686	1,813,327
2,623	2,623	2,623	2,623	2,623	2,623	2,623	31,479
928	928	928	928	928	937	928	11,145
360	360	360	360	360	370	360	4,330
427	427	427	427	427	433	427	5,130
4,338	4,338	4,338	4,338	4,338	4,366	4,338	52,084
71	71	71	71	71	71	74	855
96	96	96	96	96	96	104	1,160
--	--	--	--	--	--	--	--
142	142	142	142	142	142	148	1,710
513	513	513	513	513	512	6,155	
114	114	114	114	114	114	116	1,370
45	45	45	45	45	45	55	550
--	--	--	--	--	--	--	--
114	114	114	114	114	114	116	1,370
85	85	85	85	85	85	90	1,025
190	190	190	190	190	190	190	2,280
228	228	228	228	228	227	228	2,735
1,788	1,788	1,788	1,788	1,788	1,787	1,823	21,490

CASH FLOW BUDGET (continued)

	JANUARY	FEBRUARY	MARCH	APRIL	MAY
CONTRACT SERVICES:					
Security	2,717	2,717	2,717	2,717	2,717
Rubbish Removal	494	494	494	494	494
Snow Removal	95	95	95	95	95
Window Cleaning	95	95	95	95	95
Cleaning	4,790	4,790	4,790	4,790	4,790
Landscaping	71	71	71	71	71
Elevator	566	566	566	566	566
H.V.A.C.	712	712	712	712	712
Exterminator	35	35	35	35	35
TOTAL CONTRACT SERVICES	9,574	9,574	9,574	9,574	9,574
UTILITIES:					
Water	179	179	179	179	179
Gas	19	19	19	19	19
Electric	11,453	11,453	11,453	11,453	11,453
Steam	--	--	--	--	--
Sewer	--	--	--	--	--
TOTAL UTILITIES	11,651	11,651	11,651	11,651	11,651
ADMINISTRATIVE					
Legal	332	332	332	332	332
Accounting	475	475	475	475	475
Telephone	114	114	114	114	114
Consulting	85	85	85	85	85
Supplies	114	114	114	114	114
Management Fee	6,739	7,065	6,903	7,131	7,396
Miscellaneous	114	114	114	114	114
Insurance	3,230	3,230	3,230	3,230	3,230
Management Space	2,496	2,496	2,496	2,496	2,496
Replacements	1,140	1,140	1,140	1,140	1,140
TOTAL ADMINISTRATIVE	14,839	15,165	15,003	15,231	15,496
REAL ESTATE TAXES	19,350	19,350	19,350	19,350	19,350
TOTAL OPERATING EXPENSES	61,540	61,866	61,704	61,932	62,197
NET CASH FLOW FROM OPERATIONS	$75,873	$81,155	$77,174	$80,604	$84,727

JUNE	JULY	AUGUST	SEPTEMBER	OCTOBER	NOVEMBER	DECEMBER	TOTAL
2,717	2,717	2,717	2,717	2,717	2,717	2,718	32,605
494	494	494	494	494	494	496	5,930
95	95	95	95	95	95	95	1,140
95	95	95	95	95	95	95	1,140
4,790	4,790	4,790	4,790	4,790	4,790	4,770	57,460
71	71	71	71	71	71	74	855
565	565	565	565	565	565	555	6,770
712	712	712	712	712	712	718	8,550
35	35	35	35	35	35	25	410
9,574	9,574	9,574	9,574	9,574	9,574	9,546	114,860
179	179	179	179	179	179	181	2,150
19	19	19	19	19	19	21	230
11,453	11,453	11,453	11,453	11,453	11,453	11,457	137,440
--	--	--	--	--	--	--	--
--	--	--	--	--	--	--	--
11,651	11,651	11,651	11,651	11,651	11,651	11,659	139,820
332	332	332	332	332	332	338	3,990
475	475	475	475	475	475	475	5,700
114	114	114	114	114	114	116	1,370
85	85	85	85	85	85	90	1,025
114	114	114	114	114	114	116	1,370
7,998	8,192	8,253	7,855	7,818	7,830	8,325	91,505
114	114	114	114	114	114	116	1,370
3,230	3,230	3,230	3,230	3,230	3,230	3,230	38,760
2,496	2,496	2,496	2,496	2,496	2,496	2,496	29,952
1,140	1,140	1,140	1,140	1,140	1,140	1,140	13,680
16,098	16,292	16,353	15,955	15,918	15,930	16,442	188,722
19,350	19,350	19,350	19,350	19,350	19,350	19,350	232,200
62,799	62,993	63,054	62,656	62,619	62,658	63,158	749,176
$95,121	$97,997	$99,156	$91,365	$90,672	$90,779	$99,528	$1,064,151

LEASE SUMMARY

Lease Expiration Date	Tenant	Commencement Date	Usable Sq. Ft.	Escalation %	Rentable Sq. Ft.
01/31	XYZ Assoc.	02/01/77	594	.004165	701
03/31	Ax Grind Assoc.	04/01/75	2,055	.01440	2,425
03/31	Ax Grind Assoc. (Conference Room)	04/01/76	471	.00330	556
03/07	Four Corp.	03/08/77	5,216	.0365677	6,155
05/31	Intn'l Inc. (Best Foods)	06/01/79	992	.00696	1,171
07/31	Gen'l Corp.	06/01/77	1,456	.010207	1,718
10/31	Polar Corp.	10/15/77	31, 998	.215753	36,315
12/31	Telephone Co.	12/10/75	11,715	.0696	11,715
1981					
05/31	Water Works Assoc.	06/01/76	630	.004266	718
06/30	Cor Corp.	10/01/78	1,159	.008128	1,368
06/30	Lilly Inc.	07/01/78	1,845	.01293	2,177
06/30	Nat'l Ins. Co.	07/01/78	1,090	.0076403	1,286
08/31	Associates, Inc.	09/01/78	1,158	.00812	1,366
10/31	America Co.	11/01/78	495	.00347	584
11/30	Products Div.	12/01/78	1,725	.01169	1,967
11/30	Special Div.	12/01/78	1,795	.01216	2,046
12/31	Holiday Inc.	01/01/79	621	.004355	733
12/31	Robert Assoc.	01/01/80	2,470	.017319	2,915
1982					
01/31	Film Inc.	02/01/79	1,208	.008467	1,425
01/31	General Credit Home Branch, Inc.	02/01/79	1,516	.01027	1,728
02/28	Cap Corp.	03/01/77	479	.0033568	565
02/28	Data, Inc.	02/15/79	978	.00685	1,153
02/28	Mutual Inc.	09/01/76	3,333	.022576	3,800
03/31	Intn'l Co. (Soabar)	02/01/77	651	.00457	768
05/31	Dr. Cohen	06/01/77	1,022	.0072	1,206
06/30	Mon Company	06/15/77	821	.00576	969
07/31	Commercial Inc.	08/01/79	636	.0045331	763
10/31	Tet Inc.	11/01/79	601	.0043	721
12/31	Credit Corp.	09/01/77	2,401	.01683	2,833
1983					
04/30	Cafeteria (included common area factor)	05/01/78	4,000		
05/31	Moore Inc.	06/01/80	3,471	.02474	4,165
09/30	Ana Inc.	09/15/78	465	.003262	549
09/30	John Trust	10/01/78	670	.0047	791
12/31	Telephone Ind.	12/15/78	1,391	.00976	1,642
1984					
03/31	Telephone Service	04/01/78	6,860	.048094	8,095
04/30	Globe Insurance Corp.	04/01/79	6,943	.048676	8,193
05/31	Philip Inc.	06/01/79	2,138	.015245	2,566
07/31	Gates Co.	08/01/79	972	.006927	1,166
10/31	McDonnell Co.	11/01/79	3,630	.0259	4,356
11/30	Comm. of Mass. Probate	12/01/79	1,174	N/A	1,345
12/31	American Inc.	01/01/80	1,302	.0092801	1,562
	Roper Inc.		465	.00331	558
	Peter Co. (Management)		1,920	.01368	2,304

Base Rent Net	Annual Base	Electricity	Base Year Operating	Base Year Real Estate	Parking Space Provision	Option Term
$ 9.50	$6,660	.40	180,964.00	122,515.38	--	2 Yr. Option
8.50	20,612	.40	53,1172.65	122,515.38	use	no
8.44	4,693	.34	52,172.65	135,079.08	use	no
8.41	51,752	.40	180,963.55	142,677.97	use	2 Yr. Option
8.50	9,954	.40	153,172.65	122,515.38	use	no
8.50	14.603	.40	180,963.55	134,805.36	use	2 Yr. Option
8.50	308,678	.40	311,387.00	135,079.08	120	2 Periods of 2 Yrs
7.69	90,034	.40	153,172.65	142,677.97	65	5 Yr. Option
8.50	6,103	.40	153,172.65	135,079.08	--	no
9.89	13,530	.50	cpi Max 6%	122,515.38	3	no
9.50	20,682	.50	267,351.47	142,677.97	--	2 Yr. Option
9.50	12,217	.40	267,351.47	142,677.97	--	no
10.00	13,660	.50	267,351.47	142,677.97	--	no
10.00	5,840	.50	267,351.47	142,677.97	--	no
9.00	17,703	.50	153,172.65	180,992.09	11	no
9.00	18,414	.50	153,172.65	180,992.09	10	no
11.00	8,063	.50	301,511.89	180,992.09	--	no
8.50	24,777	.40	180,964.00	122,515.38	--	no
10.00	14,250	.50	267,351.47	142,677.97	--	2 Yr. Option
9.00	15,552	.50	153,172.65	180,992.09	5	no
8.60	4,859	.40	153,172.65	134,805.36	3	no
11.00	12,683	.50	267,351.47	180,992.09	--	3 Yr. Option, cp
8.50	32,300	.40	153,1172.65	152,935.38	--	5 Yr. Option @ $9.50/S.F.
8.50	6,528	.40	180,963.55	135,079.08	use	no
8.50	10,251	.40	180,963.55	135,079.08	--	no
8.50	8,237	.40	180,963.55	135,079.08	use	no
11.00	8,393	.50	267,351.47	214,910.48	--	3 Yr. Option
11.00	7,931	.50	153,172.65	135,079.08	use	3 Yr. Option
8.50	24,080	.40	267,351.47	142,677.97	26	3 Yr. Option
	17,600		--	--	--	--
12.50	52,063	.55		180,992.09	12	--
10.00	5,490	.50	267,351.47	142,677.97	--	no
10.00	7,910	.50	180,963.55	135,079.08	--	no
10.00	16,420	.50	402,000.00	180,992.09	--	2 Yr. Option
9.50	76,903	.40	267,351.47	135,079.08	24	no
11.00	90,123	--	402,000.00	214,910.48	3	2 Yr. Option
11.00	28,226	.50	153,172.65	135,079.08	use	no
11.00	12,826	.50	267,351.47	180,992.09	--	no
11.00	47,916	.50	267,351.47	180,992.09	--	no
11.00	14,795	N/A	N/A	N/A	4+ use of visitor parking	
11.00	17,182	.50	402,000.00			
13.00	7,254	.55	N/A			
13.00	29,952	.55	N/A			

LEASE SUMMARY (continued)

Lease Expiration Date	Tenant	Commencement Date	Usable Sq. Ft.	Escalation %	Rentable Sq. Ft.
1985					
05/31	Revere Co.	06/01/80	998	.00711	1,198
	VACANT		33,988	.242317	40,786
			151,518	1.008745	171,123

HISTORY OF OPERATION AND TAX EXPENSE USED FOR ESCALATION

	1976	1977	1978	1979
Operating Expense (1/1-12/31)	$153,173	$180,964	$267,351	$301,511
Real Estate Taxes (7/1 of preceding year through 6/30 of current year)	$122,515	$135,079	$142,678	$180,992

Base Rent Net	Annual Base	Electricity	Base Year Operating	Base Year Real Estate	Parking Space Provision	Option Term
13.00	5,574	.70	301,511.89	180,992.09		
13.00	530,218					
	$1,763,491					

CHAPTER SEVEN

Analyzing a Real Estate Investment—Real Estate Leverage

The return on investment in a real estate transaction can be dramatically increased through leverage. As we saw in our discussion of taxes, it is possible to combine investors' equity and borrowed funds and then depreciate the building from the total. This provides a tax shelter on rental income from a real estate investment. It also allows the investor to reap the appreciation from a much more significant piece of real estate than could be purchased by his equity capital alone. For example, an investor may put up $25,000, borrow $75,000, and purchase a $100,000 building with a remaining useful life of 25 years. On his own $25,000 of equity capital the transaction would not have been possible. With borrowed money, which we call leverage, the investor can make the deal and take depreciation of $4,000 (assuming no land value) per year on a 25-year straight-line schedule as an offset to income. In addition, if the whole real estate market moves up 10 percent, the profit on a $100,000 parcel will be $10,000, while the profit on a $25,000 parcel would be only $2,500. In terms of return on investment, the $10,000 profit return on $25,000 of equity is 40 percent while the $2,500 profit on the same equity is only a 10 percent return! This is the concept of leverage being used to increase the rate of return.

Of course, since leverage is debt money, it will work only as well as the terms on which it is borrowed. It is customary to think of the cost of debt in terms of the annual total of both principal and interest payments. The other important factors in using debt are the percentage charge for use of the money and the length of term over which the funds have to be repaid. In a one-year analysis of properties, the annual cost of total debt payments has to be less than the rental income for the investment to have a positive profit (also called a positive cash flow). In longer term analysis, the final cost of debt must be less than the appreciation on the property plus the sum of the yearly positive cash flows to show a final profit. The tax benefits gained by ownership will not be factored into this simple analysis.

At this point let us fix a method of calculating the yearly pretax return on investment. We shall define yearly pretax return on investment as follows:

$$\text{Yearly pretax return on investment} = \frac{\text{Net operating income} - \text{Annual mortgage principal plus interest}}{\text{Equity investment}}$$

It is easy to see that the higher the interest rates on a mortgage, the lower the percentage yearly pretax return on investment (since the numerator will decrease). However, there is also the possibility that by paying a higher rate of interest the lender will increase the term of years for repayment and thus reduce the annual amount of principal included in monthly payments. For example, Loan One is a mortgage of $100,000 at 12 percent for a term of 10 years with a repayment schedule that requires annual payments of principal and interest totalling $17,217.00. Loan Two, on the other hand, is a mortgage of $100,000 at 15 percent for a term of 20 years, requiring annual payments of principal and interest totalling $15,801.00. If we have a pretax net operating income of $20,000, and an equity investment of $25,000, the higher interest loan gives a better yearly pretax return on investment of $20,000 minus $17,217 (or $2,783), which we divide by our $25,000 equity investment to yield 11 percent. Loan Two will have a yearly pretax return on investment of $20,000 minus $15,801 (or $4,199), which we divide by our $25,000 equity investment to yield 17 percent. So in general it is apparent that the longer the length of the mortgage, the higher will be the yearly pretax return on investment, if other things remain equal.

If the cash flow of an income property declines, leverage works just as hard against the investor. There may be a sudden and alarming decrease in cash flow, and the owner may be faced with the choice of adding more equity capital or losing the property through foreclosure. If certain tax benefits have already been taken so that the owner's basis is quite low, a tax may be due even though the property is forfeited. The Internal Revenue Service will consider the unamortized amount of the loan to be the sales price and the difference between that number and the book value will produce a tax liability despite the fact that no cash is received.

Determining pretax cash flow

Figuring out the pretax cash flow of a real estate investment is rela-

CASH FLOW BUDGET
Worksheet

	Jan.	Feb.	Mar.	Apr.	May	June	July	Aug.	Sept.	Oct.	Nov.	Dec
GROSS INCOME												
Rental												
Parking												
Laundry												
Concession												
Pass through												
Percentage												
Other												
TOTAL												
EXPENSES												
Taxes (1) ____												
Taxes (2) ____												
Utilities												
Heat												
Air conditioning												
Repairs												
Maintenance												
Management												
Brokerage												
Insurance												
Other												
TOTAL												
NET OPERATING INCOME												
LESS MORTGAGE PAYMENTS												
NET PRETAX CASH FLOW												

tively uncomplicated. It is the same basic analysis that is performed in a going business. Gross income is the sum total of all sources of income from the property (i.e., rent, parking fees, laundry, concession income, rent passthrough income, percentage rent, etc.). Next, operating expenses of all kinds, such as brokerage rental fees, maintenance, utilities, taxes, insurance, sewer rent, and administration are subtracted from gross income to arrive at net operating income. Finally, we subtract the annual mortgage payments from net operating income to arrive at a net pretax cash flow amount. This simplifies our formula for yearly pretax return on investment as follows:

$$\text{Yearly pretax return on investment} = \frac{\text{Net pretax cash flow}}{\text{Equity investment}}$$

Keep in mind that yearly pretax return on investment and net pretax cash flow are related concepts. If the net pretax cash flow is a negative number, then the investor is losing money on the property. Additional funds may have to be supplied each year to make up the shortfall between gross income and operating expenses.

It is also possible that the flow of gross income and the payment of expenses during the year is not even. For example, percentage rents may only be paid twice each year and taxes may be paid monthly. This can lead to a temporary cash flow problem that forces the investor to advance sums to cover the difference from gross income and operating expenses until the percentage rent is received and the investor repaid. If the property being analyzed has a complicated income stream or expense stream, it is always an excellent idea to construct a monthly cash budget in order to be prepared for bills that must be paid out of such an irregular stream. The cash flow budget worksheet will aid you in such an analysis.

Common measurements of value

There are three accepted methods of determining the value of an income-producing property. If you need to make a quick assessment, the income approach is probably the best one to use. In a large investment, it is prudent to calculate the results from all three methods.

1. Income approach. The income approach values a property by a capitalization of the net income. The following formula is used:

$$\text{Value of property} = \frac{\text{CASH FLOW}}{\text{CAPITALIZATION RATE}}$$

The capitalization rate is the rate of return the investor requires for a particular kind of property. Such rates are arbitrary because they are fixed in the mind of the investor; they are a function of the opportunities available for alternate use of the funds. So if you feel that a 12 percent capitalization rate is required and a real estate investment has a cash flow of $50,000, we can assign a value by the following calculation:

$$\text{Value of property } (\$416{,}667) = \frac{\$50{,}000}{.12}$$

There are three fundamental problems with this income approach. First, it assumes that the cash flow will continue at its present level. It may be possible to improve cash flow significantly by increasing rents or reducing expenses. Conversely, expenses may rise dramatically through forces such as oil scarcity or tax assessment. This will decrease the numerator of our equation-- and the value of the property.

Second, income analysis totally ignores the increases in property values over time. If there are subsequent refinancings or an eventual sale, the profit may be much more significant than the investor's capitalization rate contemplated.

Finally, using a capitalization rate to figure value is rather simplistic, in that it ignores the tax consequences of the real estate investment to the individual. As we have stated several times, the tax reasons may be very important indeed!

2. Market approach. The market approach attempts to ascribe value by comparing the proposed purchase to similar properties in the area that have changed hands in recent transactions. In theory, a free market should ascribe a relatively accurate value to property. In fact, the selection of the comparables used requires astute judgment, since no two properties are truly identical. And the parties in other transactions may be guided by ulterior motives that would distort the market price.

3. Cost approach. This is an attempt to calculate what it would cost to reproduce the building in the current construction environment. The main problem with the cost approach is that materials and building techniques change over time. A new structure that will perform the identical service might realistically be built with completely different materials in an assembly-line technique at a fraction of the cost of the construction method used in an older structure.

As we can see, these measurements of value are not exact formulas. There is a margin for judgment in all three methods, and the investor must ultimately realize that there is always the risk of overpayment. Even the experts have been known to pay dearly for errors in calculating the market.

Other guides to measuring return

Free and clear return is a valuation device that enables an investor to compare various properties by removing distortions caused by different financing terms. Thus buildings of comparable size, quality, and income can be considered as places to invest limited capital. Free and clear return is determined by first adding together equity investment and all of the mortgages on the property. Then that total investment figure is plugged into the following formula:

$$\text{Free and clear return} = \frac{\text{Net operating income}}{\text{Total investment}}$$

We recall that net operating income is gross income minus expenses. Figure 7.1 below is an example of the simple computation of free and clear return. Building One has a gross rental income of $25,000, operating expenses of $15,000, and requires an equity investment of $10,000 plus a first mortgage of $50,000 and a second mortgage of $5,000. Building Two has a gross rental income of $20,000, has operating expenses of $7,000, and requires an equity investment of $9,000, in addition to a first mortgage of $50,000.

Figure 7.1

FREE AND CLEAR RETURN

	Building One	Building Two
Gross income	$25,000	$20,000
Expenses	15,000	7,000
Net operating income	$10,000	$13,000
Total investment		
Equity	$10,000	$ 9,000
First mortgage	50,000	50,000
Second mortgage	5,000	--
	$65,000	$59,000
Free and clear return	15%	22%

A high free and clear return is most desirable. When the free and clear return is low, the investor is paying more dollars for each dollar of income. The extra amount paid must be justified by the marketplace in terms of a higher quality location or more desirable and secure tenants who will enhance the value of the building.

The concept of internal rate of return (IRR) is another valuable analytical calculation commonly used by real estate investors. It is based on the idea that an amount of money that you will receive at some point in the future is worth less than money you receive today. The money you receive today will have an opportunity to earn a return in other investments until the point in the future when you would otherwise have received it. We call this relationship between time and money the net present value. The range of net present values will fluctuate, depending on how much interest we expect to earn on our money from today to that point of time in the future. Thus, we discount the future payment by a discount rate to compare it with receiving money in hand today.

For example, let us assume that you would receive $1,100 exactly one year from today. How much would you have to receive today to equal $1,100 in one year if you could earn 10 percent on that money for the next year? The answer is that you could take $1,000 today in lieu of the $1,100 one year from now. Another way of looking at the problem is to ask how much you would pay to receive $1,100 one year from now if you assume a discount rate of 10 percent. The answer is that you would pay $1,000 today if you were certain of your ability to earn 10 percent on your money.

A flow of money is a stream of earnings each year over a fixed period of years. Flows of monies as they are received each year can all be discounted to the present value. For example, the rent roll of a building over five years can be discounted when we know in advance how the rent will be increased for all tenants. Discounting the rent roll flow is how we calculate the internal rate of return. A discount rate is applied to each of the streams of flows over time, so that the aggregate net present value equals zero. The internal rate of return is the breakeven interest rate on a flow of income over time. We can compare the internal rate of return on a particular property to the internal rate of return on other investment alternatives. By making this comparison, it is fairly easy to determine how attractive it would be to employ our capital in one specific real estate investment rather than another.

It is something of a hit or miss proposition to find the discount rate that will make the net present value of an investment stream equal to zero. Discount factors are found in published tables (included on pages 150-153 of this book) and several values are applied to the stream to see how close we can get to a zero net present value. Once we get a negative net present value we know that our objective, zero, lies between that negative discount rate and the previous positive calculation. Use of a financial calculator at this point (a relatively inexpensive tool) simplifies the calculation process.

The internal rate of return in real estate is not by itself entirely useful unless we know what proportion of the investment return comes from cash flow, equity buildup, and tax shelter. These vary in each piece of real estate and an investor may prefer one form of return to another. If the return comes from the tax shelter aspect and the investor is in a low income bracket, he would not really want that property. In another case, a younger taxpayer/investor may only care about equity buildup, with cash flow a relatively unimportant aspect.

Let us examine the internal rate of return on two income properties to illustrate the concept of breaking out the three components. Building One is a small apartment house with eight units and a purchase price of $150,000. Financing is available in the amount of $125,000 for a period of 20 years at 10 percent. Building One has a gross rent roll of $23,000, operating expenses of $7,000, and the cost of yearly debt service is $12,000. Building Two is a similar ten-unit apartment house with a purchase price of $200,000. Building Two can be financed for $150,000 at 12 percent interest over a term of 25 years. Its rent roll is $27,000, from which we deduct $9,000 in operating expenses and $16,000 of yearly debt service. This information is in Figure 7.2 below.

Figure 7.2

OPERATING STATISTICS

	Building One	Building Two
Number of units	8	10
Purchase price	$150,000	$200,000
Mortgage		
Rate	10%	12%
Term	20 yrs.	25 yrs.
Amount	$125,000	$150,000
Rent roll	$23,000	$27,000
Operating expenses	7,000	9,000
Net operating income	16,000	18,000
Less mortgage payments	12,000	16,000
Pretax cash flow	$4,000	$2,000

For the sake of simplicity, we assume that both buildings may be depreciated on a straight-line basis over a period of 30 years. This would yield us $5,000 of depreciation per year on Building One and $6,666 of depreciation per year on Building Two. In the mortgage financing of Building One let us assume that $3,000 of the principal amount of the loan is amortized each year. Similarly, Building Two will repay $4,000 of principal each year in amortizing its mortgage financing.

The first step in calculating the internal rate of return is to specify our time period. Next, we must estimate the probable equity buildup that we expect to occur during that time period. For our example we shall look at a period of three years and assume that Building One will appreciate at five percent per year and Building Two will appreciate at nine percent per year. This is because Building One is in an older community where prices have more or less stabilized, while Building Two is in a nearby area where the population is increasing very rapidly. In Figure 7.3 below we will set forth a cash flow projection for the three-year time period in which we expect to hold this investment.

Figure 7.3

CASH FLOW PROJECTION FOR THREE YEAR PERIOD

BUILDING ONE

	Year 1	Year 2	Year 3
1. Pretax cash flow	$4,000	$4,000	$4,000
2. Amortization	3,000	3,000	3,000
3. Depreciation	(5,000)	(5,000)	(5,000)
4. Taxable income	2,000	2,000	2,000
5. Tax at 50% bracket	(1,000)	(1,000)	(1,000)
6. Aftertax income	$1,000	$1,000	$1,000
Aftertax cash flow (1 + 6)	$5,000	$5,000	$5,000

BUILDING TWO

	Year 1	Year 2	Year 3
1. Pretax cash flow	$2,000	$2,000	$2,000
2. Amortization	4,000	4,000	4,000
3. Depreciation	(6,666)	(6,666)	(6,666)
4. Taxable income	(666)	(666)	(666)
5. Tax benefit at 50% bracket[(A)]	333	333	333
6. Aftertax income	333	333	333
Aftertax cash flow (1 + 5)	$2,333	$2,333	$2,333

(A) A loss at taxable income level is deductible and so has a benefit to the owner of the tax savings. Here we assume a 50% tax bracket.

We now recall that our assumption was that Building One would appreciate at five percent per year and Building Two at nine precent per year. In three years of appreciation at these rates, we may sell Building One for $173,644, while the slightly larger Building Two would fetch $259,000. This completes our information; we can now set forth the streams of cash flows on each building and prepare to compute the internal rate of return. We note from Figure 7.4 that our equity investment in Building One is $25,000 ($150,000-$125,000) and in Building Two our equity investment is $50,000 ($200,000-$150,000).

Figure 7.4

STREAMS OF CASH FLOW

	Year 1	Year 2	Year 3
Building One			
Equity investment $25,000			
Annual cash flow	$5,000	$5,000	$5,000
Equity buildup (end Year 3)			$23,644
Internal rate of return 18.5%			
Building Two			
Equity investment $50,000			
Annual cash flow	$2,333	$2,333	$2,333
Equity buildup (end Year 3)			$59,000
Internal rate of return 10%			

We must now make the calculations to compute an approximate internal rate of return on each investment. We use the table of values on pages 150-153 to work the following computations on the streams of cash flow from both buildings.

To do this we take the individual cash flows in each year and discount them back to the present. Note that in the Year 0, which is the year of the transaction date, we will have a negative flow of $25,000 and $50,000 for Building One and Building Two, respectively. This represents the outflow for our initial equity investment. In each of the succeeding years we take the cash flow from Figure 7.4 and multiply it by the present value factors found in our table. Finally, we sum up the present value of all of the flows for each of the discount factors (i.e., in Building One we started at 16 percent and went to 19 percent). When the sum of the present value of the flows turns negative, that is our last time through this procedure. We then

Figure 7.5

INTERNAL RATE OF RETURN ON AFTERTAX CASH FLOW

Building One	16%	18%	18.5%	19%
Year 0 Present value	($25,000)	($25,000)	($25,000)	($25,000)
Year 1 Present value	4,310	4,235	4,225	4,195
Year 2 Present value	3,715	3,590	3,560	3,530
Year 3 Present value	18,360	17,444	17,215	17,015
Total	$ 1,385	$ 269	$ 0	$ (260)

Building Two	8%	9%	10%	10.5%
Year 0 Present value	($50,000)	($50,000)	($50,000)	($50,000)
Year 1 Present value	2,160	2,139	2,121	2,102
Year 2 Present value	1,999	1,964	1,927	1,892
Year 3 Present value	48,698	47,349	46,985	44,761
Total	$ 2,857	$ 1,452	$ 33	$(1,244)

know, in the case of Building One, that our internal rate of return lies between 18 percent and 19 percent. Through interpolation of the numbers of the present value table we arrive at 18.5 percent as a very close estimate of the IRR. The same process with Building Two shows that a 10 percent IRR is very close.

The final step in our analysis is to separate the cash flow, equity buildup, and tax shelter components of the internal rate of return. Remember, we do not simply want the highest internal rate of return but rather the transaction that offers the most appropriate return to the investor. In Figure 7.6 below we break down the components.

Figure 7.6

COMPONENTS OF INTERNAL RATE OF RETURN

UNIT	PRETAX CASH FLOW	PRESENT VALUE	EQUITY BUILDUP	PRESENT VALUE	ACTUAL TAX SHELTER	PRESENT VALUE	
Building One at IRR of 18.5%							
Year 1	$4,000	$3,376	$1,000	$ 844	0	0	
Year 2	4,000	2,848	1,000	712	0	0	
Year 3	4,000	2,404	24,644	14,811	0	0	
Total		$8,628		$16,367		0	$24,995*
Equity investment							$25,000
Building Two at IRR of 10%							
Year 1	2,000	1,818	--	--	333	303	
Year 2	2,000	1,652	--	--	333	275	
Year 3	2,000	1,502	59,000	44,309	333	250	
Total		$4,972		$44,309		$828	$50,109*
Equity investment							$50,000

*Note that due to rounding the IRR and interpolation the totals do not cancel out precisely to $25,000 for Building One and $50,000 for Building Two.

Figure 7.7

COMPONENTS OF INVESTMENT

	Building One	%	Building Two	%
Cash flow	$ 8,628	35	$ 4,972	10
Equity buildup	16,367	65	44,309	88
Actual tax shelter	0	0	828	2
Total	$24,995		$50,109	

As we can see from this exercise, in Building One the return comes entirely from cash flow and equity buildup. An investor seeking to shelter his income through real estate because he is in a high tax bracket would not be well advised to pick that particular investment. In Building Two, the component of the IRR represented by tax shelter is also quite small. Most of the IRR return in Building Two comes from equity buildup during the three-year holding period. However, the aggregate IRR of Building One is 18.5 percent as against only 10 percent on Building Two. This is such a great discrepancy that the investors probably should not agree to purchase Building Two on the terms offered. Leaving aside the desire for tax-sheltered income, Building One will return eight and a half percent more on its equity investment.

The last few pages have been directed toward a mathematical analysis of real estate investments. Formulas are good analytical tools, but they are not the only reliable method for comparing investment alternatives. The output values from mathematical analysis are only as good as your judgment in picking various discount rates, your time periods for holding the investment, and your assumption of tax impact. We shall now turn away from a strictly formula approach and do a more subjective analysis of two common forms of real estate investment. The first study will analyze the merits of purchasing a medium-size apartment building, while the second will give a framework for shopping center analysis.

Analysis of a medium-size apartment building

There are many ways to examine a real estate investment, but here is an accepted framework for judging the relative merits of a medium-size residential apartment building. What is really important in this exercise is the form of organization. Many times the broker will furnish sufficient information, but it will be up to you to piece this information together into usable form.

Example: We have been shown a 15-year-old building with an estimated remaining economic life of 35 years. The building contains 40 units, 20 of which are efficiencies renting at $180 per month, 15 are one-bedroom units renting at $300 per month, and five are two-bedroom units renting at $450 per month. The rental schedule is in line with other buildings in the area, and we are told that there is a three percent vacancy factor for the building.

You estimate (or have a professional appraiser estimate) that the land value under the building is $100,000, and you know that the price of the building is $500,000. That means that $400,000 is allocable to the building for purposes of depreciation for the new owner (a ratio of 20 percent for land and 80 percent for building). In addition to the above, we are told that the janitor's salary includes his apartment; the estimated life of appliances (refrigerators and ranges) is 12 years; a new boiler was installed two years ago at a cost of $5,400 with a 20-year guarantee, and public areas will be painted every four years while the units will be decorated every three years. The owner has given you the following statement:

Actual rent received	$118,700
Expenses:	
Insurance (3 years)	$ 1,500
Real estate taxes	17,377
Janitor's salary	8,200
Water	1,240
Electricity	1,866
Fuel (Oil #2)	9,687
New roof (15-year guarantee)	3,400
Redecorating 8 apartments	2,000
New equipment:	
4 refrigerators	900
2 ranges	450
Repairs	3,000
Supplies and miscellaneous	1,000
Painting public areas	1,800
	$52,420

We are leaving out of this example the complications of a seller's mortgage and we assume that the seller owns the building outright. Our first step in this analysis should be to organize the rental income to determine effective gross income. We define this as actual gross rent minus any vacancy allowance. In organizing the rent schedule, we should determine either a room count or a square footage count. Techniques for comparing buildings vary in different geographic areas of the country. The East seems to favor a comparison of rent income per room, while in the West they use a comparison of square foot rates on a monthly basis. In our example, let us organize on the basis of room count. An efficiency apartment has two rooms, a one-bedroom has three rooms, and a two-bedroom has four rooms. In Figure 7.8 we will construct a rent schedule by multiplying the number of each type of unit by its monthly rental value. We also determine an overall room count (105) and divide this number into gross monthly rent to determine a gross monthly rent per room. Once we know the per-room figure it is easy to compare it with other rentals in the area. You may use the newspaper to calculate other advertised rent per-room figures and see if the building's rent structure is above or below the marketplace.

One side note in our analysis--the vacancy factor in our proposed purchase is a very low three percent. This is probably indicative of a tight market where demand is outpacing supply. Therefore, a purchaser should consider raising the rentals of tenants when their leases expire. A vacancy factor of five percent with increasing rents is still quite good.

Figure 7.8

SUGGESTED FINANCIAL SCHEDULE FOR EFFECTIVE GROSS INCOME

Rental schedule	Room count	
20 efficiencies @ $180/month	20 × 2 = 40	$ 3,600
15 one-bedroom @ $300/month	15 × 3 = 45	4,500
5 two-bedroom @ $450/month	5 × 4 = 20	2,250
	105	
Gross monthly rent		$10,350
Gross monthly rent/room		98.57
Annual gross rent		124,200
Vacancy allowance		3,726
Effective gross income		$120,474

Expense items--the other side of our financial schedule--are divided into three categories: fixed charges, operating charges, and replacement reserve. The replacement reserve is really a calculation of items that will wear out and have to be replaced at some future date. Most owners do not actually set money aside in anticipation of such expenses. But the calculation tells the new owner that the income stream will be reduced by these amounts at some point in time. So if refrigerators and ranges cost $225 each and have a life of 12 years, we can expect to spend $750 per year ($225 × 40 units divided by 12 years) on each of these items. A similar calculation is made for the roof and boiler. Some real estate experts make an inspection to determine the life expectancy remaining in the items in the replacement reserve. An inspection might cause a potential purchaser to significantly increase the amounts to be set aside each year. For example, an apartment house that was built six years ago is offered for sale. If we accept a 12-year life for appliances, they have six years of remaining useful life. Thus we might want to double the rate at which the reserve is built up, setting aside $1,500 each year ($225 × 40 units divided by six years) for refrigerators and ranges.

Figure 7.9

SUGGESTED FINANCIAL SCHEDULE FOR EXPENSES

Expenses		
Fixed charges:		
Taxes, real estate	$17,377	
Insurance (1 year)	500	
		$17,877
Operating charges:		
Management @ 5% (A)	6,023	
Fuel	9,687	
Electricity	1,866	
Water	1,240	
Janitor	8,200	
Repairs	3,400	
Supplies and misc.	1,000	
Painting public areas	1,800	
Redecorating	2,000	
		35,216
Replacement reserve:		
Refrigerators ($225 × 40)/12 years	750	
Ranges ($225 × 40)/12 years	750	
Roof $3,400/15 years	227	
Boiler $5,400/18 years	300	
		2,027
Total expenses		$55,120

(A) Calculated from effective gross income.

Now we can calculate the gross income we can derive from our investment before the introduction of financing costs. Our effective gross income is $120,474 and total expenses are $55,120, which leaves $65,354 to service the mortgage and return some income to the investor.

Let us assume that the purchase price is $500,000 and the purchaser could obtain 15-year financing at 13 percent, paying interest only, for 80 percent of the purchase price. The purchaser would have to put up $100,000 of cash equity and could secure a $400,000 mortgage loan. Monthly payments on a $400,000 loan for 15 years at 13 percent (interest only) would be $4,333 (or $52,000 per year). Then we subtract this amount from the $65,354 to arrive at a cash return of $13,354 on our cash investment of $100,000.

If the building has a remaining economic life of 35 years, and we use straight-line depreciation, then each year it will have a noncash depreciation expense of $11,428 ($400,000/35 years). This will offset the $13,354 cash return and leave a taxable income of $1,926 ($13,354 - $11,428).

This purchase is obviously a great financial deal. The purchaser puts up $100,000 and receives an 11.4 percent ($11,428/$100,000) tax-free income stream as well as a $1,926 taxable income stream. In addition, any appreciation on the building will be realized by the purchaser on resale.

Shopping center analysis

The evaluation of purchasing or constructing a shopping center is quite a complex matter. In either situation it is advisable to have a general feasibility study that attempts to set forth a projection of the profit opportunities for the project. In the case of an existing center, such a study should focus on historical data and the potential to increase rental income, expansion by virtue of a growing marketplace, attracting better tenants, and capturing a larger percentage of the retail shopping in the area. If the project involves new construction, then the scope of the feasibility study should be expanded. Since no historical operating data will be available, access to the site, population trends of the trade area, local zoning problems, competition, and a host of other factors need to be considered. Many firms have the expertise to perform a feasibility study; your real estate adviser can recommend one in your area.

Tenant characteristics are an important component of the value of a shopping center. Strong tenants attract customers who, in turn, create the potential for substantial rent increases on lease renewal. Aside from fixed rent escalation, a busy shopping center pays off heavily in percentage rent overrides. Such overrides are different for each tenant classification and operational type. The most common tenant classifications, percentage rents, and types of tenants are set forth in Figure 7.10 below.

Figure 7.10

CLASSIFICATION OF TENANTS, PERCENTAGE RENT, AND TYPE

Classification	Percentage rent
Automotive	4 - 6%
Garden supplies	6 - 9%
Building materials	4 - 6%
General merchandise	2 - 5%
Food	1 - 1½%
Food service	2 - 3%
Clothing	5 - 8%
Shoes	7 - 10%
Hardware	4 - 6%
Hobbies	6 - 10%

Home furnishings	3 - 6%
Home appliances	3 - 5%
Jewelry	5 - 10%
Cosmetics	4 - 6%
Liquor	3 - 5%
Drugs	$2\frac{1}{2}$ - 4%
Optical	8 - 10%
Personal services	4 - 6%
Dry cleaning	7 - 8%
Books	7 - 9%
Restaurant	5 - 7%

Type

National chain
Regional chain
Local chain
Independent

There are four different types of shopping centers as defined by the International Council of Shopping Centers. The first is the super regional center, which is a very large business area equivalent to the central business district of a major market. The average total area of a super regional center is about 993,000 square feet and there are at least three major department stores with gross leased area of 100,000 or more square feet. The next step down is the regional center, which has a depth and variety of shopping comparable to a small city business district. This means that a regional center has about 581,000 square feet of gross leasable area with two major department stores of at least 100,000 square feet.

The third category is the community center, offering a wide range of facilities with the major tenant being a small department store or a discount department store. The average size for a community center is around 162,000 feet. The fourth and smallest category of shopping center is the neighborhood center with an average of 54,000 square feet. A neighborhood center supplies the daily living needs of the surrounding population and is often anchored by a supermarket.

In the following worksheet the basic information for constructing a new shopping center or purchasing an existing one can be assembled. It is not within the scope of this book to attempt a full financial analysis of all of the variables that enter into a complex shopping center study. However, the worksheet will clarify important elements and help determine if it is worthwhile to hire a professional to undertake a feasibility study. You should weigh the return on cash and return on investment results against your own portfolio requirements; and then factor in real estate management.

Figure 7-11

SHOPPING CENTER WORKSHEET

PRO FORMA

1. LAND	
Total square feet of land	______ sq. ft.
Building area on land	______ sq. ft.
Walkways	______ sq. ft.
Signs	______ sq. ft.
Parking area	______ sq. ft.
Unused land	______ sq. ft.
Estimated cost of land	$ ______
Divided by: total square feet of land	______ sq. ft.
Equals: cost per square foot	$ ______
2. CONSTRUCTION COSTS	
Grading and site preparation	$ ______
Sewer hookup	______
Foundation	______
Building shell	______
Building interior	______
Parking lot paving	______
Amenities	
1) Lighting	______
2) Walkways	______
3) Out structures	______
Permits	______
Other	______
TOTAL	$ ______
3. PROFESSIONAL FEES	
Advertising and promotion	$ ______
Accounting	______
Architect	______
Engineering	______
Brokerage	______
Legal	______
Other	______
TOTAL	$ ______
4. INTERIM FINANCING	
Closing costs	$ ______
Commitment fees	______
Other financing fees	______
TOTAL	$ ______

Total interim estimated cost	$ ________
Less: construction loans	________
Equals: interim cash required	$ ________

5. PERMANENT FINANCING

Total estimated cost	$ ________
Less: mortgage financing	$ ________
Equals: cash required	$ ________
Yearly debt service amount	$ ________

6. INCOME AND EXPENSE

INCOME	Gross	Per square foot
Fixed minimum rent	$	$
Percentage rent/overrides		
Common facilities		
Real estate taxes		
Mall HVAC		
Tenant HVAC		
Other	$ ________	$ ________
Less: allowance for vacancy	________	________
(A) Gross income		

OPERATING EXPENSES	Gross	Per square foot
Management cost (general)		
Management cost (on site)		
Advertising & promotion		
Insurance		
Real estate taxes		
Remodeling		
Maintenance		
Miscellaneous		
(B) Total operating expenses	$ ________	$ ________
NET SURPLUS FOR DEBT SERVICE (A - B)	$ ________	$ ________

7. RETURN TO INVESTOR(S)

RETURN ON CASH

Net surplus for debt service	$ __________
Minus: yearly debt service amount	$ __________
Equals: NET OPERATING PROFIT	$ __________

RETURN ON CASH

Net operating profit	$ __________
Divided by: cash required	$ __________
Equals: RETURN ON CASH	__________ %

RETURN ON INVESTMENT

Net operating profit	$ __________
Plus: mortgage amortization	__________
Equals: combined return	$ __________
Combined return	$ __________
Divided by: total estimated cost	__________
Equals: return on investment	__________ %

PRESENT VALUE FACTORS

Table I: PRESENT VALUE OF ONE DOLLAR AT THE END OF n YEARS

Year (n)	1%	2%	3%	4%	5%	6%	7%	8%	9%	10%	12%	14%	15%	Year (n)
1	0.990	0.980	0.970	0.962	952	0.943	0.935	0.926	0.917	0.909	0.893	0.977	0.870	1
2	0.980	0.961	0.943	0.925	0.907	0.890	0.873	0.857	0.842	0.826	0.797	0.769	0.756	2
3	0.971	0.942	0.915	0.889	0.864	0.840	0.816	0.794	0.772	0.751	0.712	0.675	0.658	3
4	0.961	0.924	0.888	0.855	0.823	0.792	0.763	0.735	0.708	0.683	0.636	0.592	0.572	4
5	0.951	0.906	0.863	0.822	0.784	0.747	0.713	0.681	0.650	0.621	0.567	0.519	0.497	5
6	0.942	0.888	0.837	0.790	0.746	0.705	0.666	0.630	0.596	0.564	0.507	0.456	0.432	6
7	0.933	0.871	0.813	0.760	0.711	0.665	0.623	0.583	0.547	0.513	0.452	0.400	0.376	7
8	0.923	0.863	0.789	0.731	0.677	0.627	0.582	0.540	0.502	0.467	0.404	0.361	0.327	8
9	0.914	0.837	0.766	0.703	0.645	0.592	0.544	0.500	0.460	0.424	0.361	0.308	0.284	9
10	0.905	0.820	0.744	0.676	0.614	0.558	0.508	0.463	0.422	0.386	0.322	0.270	0.247	10
11	0.896	0.804	0.722	0.660	0.585	0.527	0.475	0.429	0.388	0.350	0.287	0.237	0.215	11
12	0.887	0.788	0.701	0.625	0.557	0.497	0.444	0.397	0.356	0.319	0.257	0.208	0.187	12
13	0.879	0.773	0.681	0.601	0.530	0.469	0.415	0.368	0.326	0.290	0.229	0.182	0.163	13
14	0.870	0.758	0.661	0.577	0.505	0.442	0.388	0.340	0.299	0.263	0.205	0.160	0.141	14
15	0.861	0.743	0.642	0.555	0.481	0.417	0.362	0.315	0.275	0.239	0.183	0.140	0.123	15
16	0.853	0.728	0.623	0.534	0.458	0.394	0.339	0.299	0.252	0.218	0.163	0.123	0.107	16
17	0.844	0.714	0.605	0.513	0.436	0.371	0.317	0.270	0.231	0.198	0.146	0.108	0.093	17
18	0.836	0.700	0.587	0.494	0.416	0.350	0.296	0.250	0.212	0.180	0.130	0.095	0.081	18
19	0.828	0.686	0.570	0.475	0.396	0.331	0.277	0.232	0.194	0.164	0.116	0.083	0.070	19
20	0.820	0.673	0.554	0.456	0.377	0.312	0.258	0.215	0.178	0.149	0.104	0.073	0.061	20
21	0.811	0.660	0.538	0.439	0.369	0.294	0.242	0.199	0.164	0.135	0.093	0.064	0.053	21
22	0.803	0.647	0.522	0.422	0.342	0.278	0.226	0.184	0.150	0.123	0.083	0.056	0.046	22
23	0.795	0.634	0.507	0.406	0.326	0.262	0.211	0.170	0.138	0.112	0.074	0.049	0.040	23
24	0.788	0.622	0.492	0.390	0.310	0.247	0.197	0.158	0.126	0.102	0.066	0.043	0.035	24
25	0.780	0.610	0.478	0.375	0.295	0.233	0.184	0.146	0.116	0.092	0.059	0.038	0.030	25

Year (n)	16%	18%	20%	22%	24%	25%	26%	28%	30%	35%	40%	50%	Year (n)
1	0.862	0.847	0.833	0.820	0.806	0.800	0.794	0.781	0.769	0.741	0.714	0.667	1
2	0.743	0.718	0.694	0.672	0.650	0.640	0.630	0.610	0.592	0.549	0.510	0.444	2
3	0.641	0.609	0.579	0.551	0.524	0.512	0.500	0.477	0.455	0.406	0.364	0.296	3
4	0.552	0.516	0.482	0.451	0.423	0.410	0.397	0.373	0.350	0.301	0.260	0.198	4
5	0.476	0.437	0.402	0.370	0.341	0.328	0.315	0.291	0.269	0.223	0.186	0.132	5
6	0.410	0.370	0.333	0.303	0.275	0.262	0.250	0.227	0.207	0.165	0.133	0.088	6
7	0.354	0.314	0.279	0.249	0.222	0.210	0.198	0.178	0.159	0.122	0.095	0.059	7
8	0.305	0.266	0.233	0.204	0.179	0.168	0.157	0.139	0.123	0.091	0.068	0.039	8
9	0.263	0.225	0.194	0.167	0.144	0.134	0.125	0.108	0.094	0.067	0.048	0.026	9
10	0.227	0.191	0.162	0.137	0.116	0.107	0.099	0.085	0.073	0.050	0.035	0.017	10
11	0.195	0.162	0.135	0.112	0.094	0.086	0.079	0.066	0.056	0.037	0.025	0.012	11
12	0.168	0.137	0.112	0.092	0.076	0.069	0.062	0.052	0.043	0.027	0.018	0.008	12
13	0.145	0.116	0.093	0.075	0.061	0.055	0.050	0.040	0.033	0.020	0.013	0.005	13
14	0.125	0.099	0.078	0.062	0.049	0.044	0.039	0.032	0.025	0.015	0.009	0.003	14
15	0.108	0.084	0.065	0.051	0.040	0.035	0.031	0.025	0.020	0.011	0.006	0.002	15
16	0.093	0.071	0.054	0.042	0.032	0.028	0.025	0.019	0.015	0.008	0.005	0.002	16
17	0.080	0.060	0.045	0.034	0.026	0.023	0.020	0.015	0.012	0.006	0.003	0.001	17
18	0.069	0.051	0.038	0.028	0.021	0.018	0.016	0.012	0.009	0.005	0.002	0.001	18
19	0.060	0.043	0.031	0.023	0.017	0.014	0.012	0.009	0.007	0.003	0.002		19
20	0.051	0.037	0.026	0.019	0.014	0.012	0.010	0.007	0.005	0.002	0.001		20
21	0.044	0.031	0.022	0.015	0.011	0.009	0.008	0.006	0.004	0.002	0.001		21
22	0.038	0.026	0.018	0.013	0.009	0.007	0.006	0.004	0.003	0.001	0.001		22
23	0.033	0.022	0.015	0.010	0.007	0.006	0.005	0.003	0.002	0.001			23
24	0.028	0.019	0.013	0.008	0.006	0.005	0.004	0.003	0.002	0.001			24
25	0.024	0.016	0.010	0.007	0.005	0.004	0.003	0.002	0.001	0.001			25

From Ezra Solomon, John J. Pringle, An Introduction to Financial Management. ©1977, Goodyear Publishing Company.

PRESENT VALUE FACTORS

Table II: PRESENT VALUE OF ONE DOLLAR PER YEAR FOR n YEARS

Year (n)	1%	2%	3%	4%	5%	6%	7%	8%	9%	10%	12%	14%	15%	Year (n)
1	0.990	0.980	0.971	0.962	0.952	0.943	0.935	0.926	0.917	0.909	0.893	0.377	0.870	1
2	1.970	1.942	1.914	1.886	1.859	1.833	1.808	1.783	1.759	1.736	1.690	1.647	1.626	2
3	2.941	2.884	2.829	2.775	2.723	2.673	2.624	2.577	2.531	2.487	2.402	2.322	2.283	3
4	3.902	3.808	3.717	3.630	3.546	3.465	3.387	3.312	3.240	3.170	3.037	2.914	2.855	4
5	4.854	4.713	4.580	4.452	4.330	4.212	4.100	3.993	3.890	3.791	3.605	3.433	3.352	5
6	5.796	5.601	5.417	5.242	5.076	4.917	4.767	4.623	4.486	4.365	4.111	3.889	3.785	6
7	6.728	6.472	6.230	6.002	5.786	5.582	5.389	5.206	5.033	4.868	4.564	4.288	4.160	7
8	7.652	7.325	7.020	6.733	6.463	6.210	5.971	5.747	5.535	5.335	4.968	4.639	4.487	8
9	8.566	8.162	7.786	7.435	7.108	6.802	6.515	6.247	5.985	5.759	5.328	4.946	4.772	9
10	9.471	8.983	8,530	8.111	7.722	7.360	7.024	6.710	6.481	6.145	5.650	5.218	5.019	10
11	10.368	9.787	9.253	8.760	8.306	7.887	7.499	7.139	6.805	6.495	5.938	5.453	5.234	11
12	11.255	10.575	9.954	9.385	8.863	8.384	7.943	7.536	7.161	6.814	6.194	5.660	5.421	12
13	12.134	11.348	10.635	9.986	9.394	8.853	8.358	7.904	7.487	7.103	6.424	5.842	5.583	13
14	13.004	12.106	11.296	10.563	9.899	9.295	8.745	8.244	7.786	7.367	6.628	6.002	5.725	14
15	13.865	12.849	11.938	11.118	10.380	9.712	9.108	8.560	8.061	7.606	6.811	6.142	5.847	15
16	14.718	13.578	12.561	11.652	10.838	10.106	9.447	8.851	8.313	7.824	6.974	6.265	5.954	16
17	15.562	14.292	13.166	12.166	11.274	10.477	9.763	9.122	8.544	8.022	7.120	6.373	6.047	17
18	16.398	14.992	13.753	12.659	11.690	10.828	10.059	9.372	8.756	8.201	7.250	6.467	6.128	18
19	17.226	15.678	14.324	13.134	12.085	11.158	10.336	9.604	8.950	8.365	7.366	6.550	6.198	19
20	18.046	16.351	14.877	13.590	12.462	11.470	10.594	9.818	9.129	8.514	7.469	6.623	6.259	20
21	18.857	17.011	15.415	14.029	12.821	11.764	10.836	10.017	9.292	8.649	7.56	6.687	6.313	21
22	19.661	17.658	15.937	14.451	13,163	12.042	11.061	10.201	9.442	8.772	7.645	6.743	6.359	22
23	20.456	18.292	16.444	14.857	13,489	12.303	11.272	10.371	9.580	8.883	7.718	6.792	6.399	23
24	21.244	18.914	16.936	15.247	13.799	12.550	11.469	10.529	9.707	8.985	7.784	6.835	6.434	24
25	22.023	19.523	17.413	15,622	14.094	12.783	11.654	10.675	9.823	9.077	7.843	6.873	6.464	25

Year (n)	16%	18%	20%	22%	24%	25%	26%	28%	30%	35%	40%	50	Year (n)
1	0.862	0.848	0.833	0.820	0.807	0.800	0.794	0.781	0.769	0.741	0.714	0.667	1
2	1.605	1.566	1.528	1.492	1.457	1.440	1.424	1.392	1.361	1.289	1.225	1.111	2
3	2.246	2.174	2.107	2.042	1.981	1.952	1.923	1.868	1.816	1.696	1.589	1.407	3
4	2.798	2.690	2.589	2.494	2.404	2.362	2.320	2.241	2.166	1.997	1.849	1.605	4
5	3.274	3.127	2.991	2.864	2.745	2.689	2.635	2.532	2.436	2.220	2.935	1.737	5
6	3.685	3.498	3.326	3.167	3.021	2.951	2.885	2.759	2.643	2.385	2.168	1.824	6
7	4.039	3.812	3.605	3.416	3.242	3.161	3.083	2.937	2.802	2.508	2.263	1.883	7
8	4.344	4.078	3.837	3.619	3.421	3.329	3.241	3.076	2.925	2.598	2.331	1.922	8
9	4.607	4.303	4.031	3.786	3.566	3.463	3.366	3.184	3.019	2.665	2.379	1.948	9
10	4.833	4.494	4.193	3.923	3.682	3.571	3.465	3.269	3.092	2.715	2.414	1.965	10
11	5.029	4.656	4.327	4.035	3.776	3.656	3.544	3.335	3.147	2.752	2.438	1.977	11
12	5.197	4.793	4.439	4.127	3.851	3.725	3.606	3.387	3.190	2.779	2.456	1.985	12
13	5.342	4.910	4.533	4.203	3.912	3.780	3.656	3.427	3.223	2.799	2.469	1.990	13
14	5.468	5.008	4.611	4.265	3.962	3.824	3.695	3.459	3.249	3.814	2.478	1.993	14
15	5.575	5.092	4.676	4.315	4.001	3.859	3.726	3.483	3.268	2.826	2.484	1.995	
16	5.669	5.162	4.730	4.357	4.033	3.887	3.751	3.503	3.283	2.834	2.489	1.997	16
17	5.749	5.222	4.775	4.391	4.059	3.910	3.771	3.518	3.295	2.840	2.492	1.998	17
18	5.818	5.273	4.812	4.419	4.080	3.928	3.786	3.529	3.304	2.844	2.494	1.999	18
19	5.878	5.316	4.844	4.442	4.097	3.942	3.799	3.539	3.311	2.848	2.496	1.999	19
20	5.929	5.353	4.870	4.460	4.110	3.954	3.808	3.546	3.316	2.850	2.497	1.999	20
21	5.973	5.384	4.891	4.476	4.121	3.963	3.816	3.551	3.320	2.852	2.498	2.000	21
22	6.011	5.410	4.909	4.488	4.130	3.971	3.822	3.556	3.323	2.853	2.499	2.000	22
23	6.044	5.432	4.925	4.499	4.137	3.976	3.827	3.559	3.325	2.854	2.499	2.000	23
24	6.073	5.451	4.937	4.507	4.143	3.981	3.831	3.562	3.327	2.855	2.499	2.000	24
25	6.097	5.467	4.948	4.514	4.147	3.985	3.834	3.564	3.329	2.856	2.499	2.000	25

CHAPTER EIGHT

Financing Investment Property

In the preceding material we discussed the importance of proper leverage in an investment property. Now we shall turn to the specifics of judging the viability of a particular project and picking the most appropriate form of mortgage debt. To do this, we shall first discuss the most common sources of borrowed funds in the current marketplace. The availability of funds from a particular category of lender will vary with factors such as the geographical location of the property, the size of the transaction, the credit of the borrower, state regulations on lending, and the general availability of liquidity in the marketplace. Because there are few hard and fast rules, it is prudent to check with several potential sources of funds to obtain a favorable rate and the most flexible terms and conditions.

Commercial banks are probably the most common source of funds for a real estate investment. In many states commercial banks lend on real estate properties as small as an owner-occupied single-family house, and as large as a super-regional shopping center. The problem with commercial banks is that they are boxed in by a maze of federal and state regulations that prohibit certain kinds of lending or else limit the loan amounts available.

The first step in developing a financing strategy is to visit the mortgage department of a commercial bank in your area and explore the kinds of loans they are permitted and willing to make. Ask if they would welcome more of your particular type of business to be certain that external market conditions have not led commercial banks to lose interest in real estate mortgages. On the whole, because the commercial mortgage bankers are sophisticated lenders in all types of real estate, they can prove to be a valuable source of information on structuring complex transactions.

Mutual savings banks are state-chartered thrift institutions that are common in the Northeast and Mid-Atlantic areas. They are traditionally a source of residential mortgages for their depositors. If you are considering buying single-family houses and renting them, mutual savings banks might be a source of financing. The residential home is a type of property they feel comfortable with, and if they know the marketplace their advice is liable to be useful. However, many mutual savings banks will only offer a home mortgage if the borrower plans to make the property his primary residence.

Savings and loan associations are both state and federally chartered and exist in all 50 states. They hold more real estate mortgages than any other form of lender. Unfortunately, they too are directed chiefly toward residential mortgages and rarely become involved in a commercial project.

Life insurance companies are an excellent source of financing for larger real estate ventures. These companies have a large cash flow coming in from policy-holder premiums, which they seek to invest in real estate mortgages. They will often make the short-term construction loan if they can also extend the long-term permanent loan. On the whole, life insurance companies seek out mortgage loans with terms of 15 to 25 years. The mortgage department of a medium to large life insurance company is constantly studying highly complex real estate transactions. Thus, they can be a valuable source for researching alternative financing strategies. And once you have built up a good track record with insurance companies, it will obviously be much easier for you to finance larger and more sophisticated deals.

Mortgage brokers (bankers) exist in most financial centers throughout the United States. They are intermediaries, like real estate brokers, who match up the developer/purchaser with the most appropriate loan source. A mortgage broker charges a fee between one-half and five percent of the money raised through his efforts. The amount charged will depend on several variables, including the size of the project, credit of the borrower, type of property, location, and terms and conditions desired by the borrower. Sometimes a mortgage broker will service the loan for the lender by receiving the periodic payments and enforcing conditions such as adequate insurance and prompt payment of real estate taxes on the mortgaged property. It is not uncommon for a mortgage broker to combine several loans in one package to create a more attractive loan for large lenders such as insurance companies and pension funds. These sources of money may well be outside the geographic region in which the real estate is situated.

Pension funds are a major source of lendable real estate funds. However, they rarely deal directly with an individual promoter because pension funds must put large amounts of money to work. The average investor can't attempt transactions of such magnitude as to interest pension fund managers. Thus, your best route to pension fund financing is through a mortgage broker who, as we noted above, packages many loans in a unit that would be substantial enough to attract a particular pension fund. Like the insurance companies, the pension funds tend to be long-term lenders who want a secure return on their investment. Lower-risk transactions are, by and large, the only thing they will consider.

Aside from these primary sources of funds, there are other secondary avenues open to the entrepreneur. These include local retirement funds, credit unions, real estate investment trusts, mortgage companies, and private individuals. As a practical matter, the easiest of these to attract is the wealthy private individual who is seeking a safe return on his capital. It is possible to place ads in financial publications such as _The Wall Street Journal_ and attract such investors. Sometimes the investor will stipulate some form of equity participation in the project. However, if his funds make the real estate investment possible, this extra cost for money may be a relatively small price to pay.

One side note. It is advisable to have an attorney represent you in securing mortgage debt. The wording of the loan document can be crucial if everything does not progress exactly as planned. Banks and other lenders are aware that there is some room for flexibility in the covenants and conditions which go along with the extension of credit. Experienced legal counsel can be very helpful in knowing where and how concessions can be obtained. Even the most sophisticated borrowers find it well worth the cost to have expert advice in this stage of a real estate investment.

Key types of financing

The most common type of mortgage loan is the conventional credit agreement for a fixed-rate, self-amortizing loan. This means that the cost of credit in terms of interest expense does not vary during the life of the loan even if money market rates fluctuate. Self-amortizing means that the borrower makes periodic payments of principal, which are computed to reduce the balance outstanding to zero when the last payment is made. Since each periodic payment is a fixed amount for each installment, the division between applying the payment to principal and interest will change constantly. In the early years almost all of the payment will cover interest costs. As time goes on, and principal is repaid, the proportion changes. There will eventually come a point where most of the payment will be applied to principal.

Since interest expense is a deductible item in our tax system, the early period of a fixed-rate, self-amortizing loan provides a larger tax deduction. Therefore, most real estate investors prefer to refinance a loan at the point where principal repayments become a major portion of the installment payment. Below, in Figure 8.1, is a table setting forth the percentage of loan principal remaining for various interest rates and maturities of loans. The percent equity buildup in a particular mortgage will be the difference between the loan principal remaining and 100 percent.

Figure 8.1

Interest rate	5 years	10 years	15 years	20 years	25 years	30 years
		Loan remaining after				
		Life of mortgage - 30 years				
7%	94%	86%	74%	57%	33%	0%
7½	95	87	75	59	34	0
8	95	88	77	60	36	0
9	96	89	79	63	39	0
10	97	91	82	66	41	0
		Life of mortgage - 25 years				
7%	91%	79%	61%	36%	0%	
7½	92	80	62	37	0	
8	92	81	64	38	0	
9	93	83	66	40	0	
10	94	85	69	43	0	
		Life of mortgage - 20 years				
7%	86%	67%	39%	0%		
7½	87	68	40	0		
8	87	79	41	0		
9	89	71	43	0		
10	90	73	45	0		

A variation of the fixed-rate, self-amortizing loan is designed to meet the needs of a borrower who prefers to make smaller monthly payments. One or more of the mortgage payments can be designed to be much larger than the regular periodic installment. Such a loan is called a balloon mortgage, and the larger installments are referred to as balloon payments. In the most common types of balloon mortgage, the final payment includes a large portion of the principal borrowed. Lenders will extend this kind of credit to a borrower who appears capable of meeting the large final payment, or to an investment that is almost certain to be refinanced long before the final payment is due. The effect of deferring repayment of a substantial portion of the principal is twofold. First, interest expense goes up, since more borrowed funds will be outstanding during the life of the loan. But that's acceptable to the borrower, since interest is a deductible expense. Second, the gross amount of the periodic payment will often be reduced. This helps raise the return on investment realized by the borrower, because more income is available after debt service.

Standby commitments are used by builders to hedge against the increasing cost of borrowing. It is an option to borrow money at a fixed rate, for a fixed term, at a future time. There is usually a nonrefundable commitment fee of one to three percent of the mortgage amount; and sometimes a deposit is required. A standby commitment puts the builder in a position of strength, from which he can negotiate with other lenders if he so desires. The builder has the security of a guaranteed source of money in the event that he cannot obtain a mortgage on more favorable terms and conditions. The small initial costs of a standby commitment can be recouped many times over if the borrower can leverage himself into a slight interest saving on a long-term loan with another lender. The lender in a standby commitment does not really plan to make the loan. However, in times of tight credit it is possible that the loan would have to be funded.

Construction loans are funds advanced during the building or renovation of properties. This is short-term money that the lender expects to be repaid by the participation of the ultimate long-term lender. Such repayment is called the takeout. At one time it was possible to obtain a construction loan without a takeout, but this is now virtually impossible. Construction lenders do not want a long-term loan, and without an ultimate mortgage lender they run the risk of being indefinitely committed to a project. The construction loan will probably run for two or three years, at a high interest rate, and with personal liability on the part of the borrower. In general, there is no penalty for prepayment at an earlier date.

Rates of interest on a construction loan are generally set on a prime plus constant basis. In times of rapidly rising interest rates the high charges on a floating construction loan can severely crimp the cash flow of the builder/investor.

The wraparound mortgage is used for the sale of existing properties that are owned subject to mortgages. In many cases the interest rates on these older mortgages are lower than the current market rates. This makes the old mortgages valuable in themselves, because current rates would make similar amounts of financing more expensive. In a wraparound mortgage the seller retains the obligation to pay the old mortgage even after the sale. The buyer then executes a wraparound mortgage, which is subordinated to the existing mortgage with interest and amortization payments at the current market rates. For example, a building is being sold for $200,000. It has an assumable mortgage of $100,000 at seven percent with 20 years to run. The buyer has cash equity of only $40,000. In addition, current market interest rates for similar mortgages are at 11 percent. The seller can keep the $100,000 mortgage at seven percent and extend to the purchaser a $160,000 mortgage at 11 percent. On the first $100,000 portion the seller will make a four point interest spread profit--the difference between his interest cost of seven percent and the 11 percent he is charging the seller. The property itself and the $40,000 cash down payment are collateral for the wraparound mortgage.

In many ways the wraparound mortgage is very much like a second mortgage. The seller in our example is extending credit above the $100,000 of previously obtained mortgage money to bring about the sale. In doing so the seller remains liable on the original $100,000 mortgage and has the risk of being paid out on the additional $60,000 of credit extended to the buyer. With rising interest rates lending institutions have attempted to put a damper on this type of activity. Most mortgages have an alienation or acceleration clause providing for the termination of the underlying existing mortgage when the property changes owners. Further, many sellers prefer not to be liable on a mortgage to a lender when they no longer control the management and use of the property. If the new owner suffers reverses and stops his payments, the seller would have to advance his own funds to protect his wraparound mortgage. Failure to do so would provoke a default on the old mortgage with possible foreclosure and sale of the property at a depressed price.

Variable rate mortgages are a recent innovation in the mortgage field; they came into being as inflation proved to be persistent. Long-term fixed rate loans often had to be discounted as interest costs on current mortgages rose well above what was charged in previous mortgage transactions. In a variable rate mortgage, interest rates are not fixed permanently. Rather, they are allowed to change to reflect current market conditions. The interest on a variable rate mortgage is tied to an agreed-upon index and is periodically adjusted upward or reduced as warranted by movements in the index. The magnitude of movements is restricted to prevent radical shifts. Most variable rate mortgages are currently limited to a one-half to one percent shift in any year and two and one-half to four percent over the entire mortgage life. Not all states allow the variable rate mortgages and most such mortgages have been made for single family houses.

But as inflation continues to erode the value of portfolios of fixed rate mortgages, many experts foresee wider use of the variable rate concept.

The graduated-payment mortgage is another relatively new lending form used almost exclusively in the single family residence. It is based on the assumption that a person will increase his earning power over the life of his career. Thus he will be able to make larger mortgage payments as his income increases, without significantly affecting his lifestyle.

In a graduated-payment mortgage there are three ways to increase payments. The interest rate remains constant while the amount of principal repaid is increased; or the interest rate is increased over time but the principal repaid periodically remains fixed; finally, both the amount of principal and the interest rate can be adjusted during the life of the loan.

Purchase money mortgages, often called "second mortgages," are a common part of real estate finance. In a purchase money mortgage the seller accepts an interest-bearing note for a part of the purchase price and secures the note with the property. There is a primary mortgage, called a "first mortgage," extended by another lender, that covers the bulk of the buyer's financing needs. In case of a default, the first mortgage is entitled to be repaid out of the proceeds of sale of the property before any funds are applied to repay the second mortgage. Because of the additional element of risk in the purchase money mortgage, it should command a higher rate of interest and a shorter repayment schedule. It is not uncommon to find a first mortgage with a term of 15 to 20 years, while the purchase money mortgage must be amortized in five to 10 years. If there is a possibility that a buyer might not derive as much income from the property as the seller, a seller may insist on further protection of his second mortgage position through various kinds of insurance (such as rental income insurance), or a demand for additional collateral, or a personal guarantee.

Cap rates and loan constants

Investment-grade income properties should have a positive cash flow. This means that rental income should exceed expenditures on a pretax basis. A positive cash flow helps protect an investor against unexpected changes in expenses or income. For example, in 1979 some landlords found that the cost of fuel oil for heating doubled in a single year. Without a cushion of positive cash flow the increased expenditure would have to be met immediately by sizable new cash outlays.

The cash flow received from an income property is measured by comparing the capitalization rate (cap rate) and a loan constant. The cap rate is the net operating income, divided by the purchase price, shown as follows:

$$\text{CAP RATE} = \frac{\text{NET OPERATING INCOME}}{\text{PURCHASE PRICE}}$$

So a property with net operating income of $20,000 which cost $200,000 has a cap rate of 10 percent ($20,000 divided by $200,000). The loan constant is the yearly loan payments of principal on the property. The formula is:

$$\text{LOAN CONSTANT} = \frac{\text{YEARLY PRINCIPAL + INTEREST}}{\text{ORIGINAL PRINCIPAL}}$$

So if the property above had a mortgage of $150,000 at 12 percent for a period of 30 years, the monthly payments of $1,542.92 times 12 months equals $18,515.04. Dividing the yearly loan payment of $18,515.04 by the principal amount of $150,000, we come up with a loan constant of 12.3 percent.

You will have a negative cash flow when the cap rate is less than the loan constant. Here our cap rate is 10 percent and our loan constant is 12.3 percent, so we can expect to see a negative cash flow. The problem can be remedied by either increasing our cap rate or decreasing the loan constant. Some guidelines for doing this are:

Increasing cap rates

1. Invest in an area where property sells at a lower price in relation to its income.
2. Select property with lower than market rents that may subsequently be raised.
3. Manage the property more effectively to cut costs.
4. Seek larger properties that tend to have a better positive cash flow.

Decreasing loan constant

1. Try to obtain financing with one or more balloons.
2. Get the seller to provide some cheaper financing to beef up the cash flow.
3. Find a graduated payment mortgage and sell before the switch over from positive to negative cash flow.
4. Get a lower constant government loan if it is available.

Keep in mind, however, that it may still pay to buy a property with some negative cash flow. The after-tax consequence may make the situation net out as a reasonable opportunity. If you feel that real estate is on an upward curve, everything might work out well as long as you don't overextend and get caught in a cash flow squeeze. Have enough financial reserves to cover any negative cash flow, as if the tax benefits did not exist.

Sale and leaseback

Sale and leaseback is a transaction whereby the seller transfers title to his property to the buyer and simultaneously leases the property back for a specified period of time. The advantage to the seller/lessee is that he can deduct the entire lease payment as a regular business expense. When he owned the property and made mortgage payments, only the interest portion of his periodic payments was deductible. The seller also frees up his cash equity in the property; further, the lease obligation does not have to be shown on the company balance sheet if the seller is a business. On the other hand, the seller loses his deduction for depreciation, as well as a chance to realize a gain on the market appreciation of the property over time.

The buyer in a sale and leaseback transaction gains all the tax shelter benefits of a real estate investment, along with a built-in long-term tenant, with, presumably, some financial strength. In addition, sometimes the buyer might be able to resell the property at the expiration of the lease at its appreciated value. His main risk in a sale and leaseback is the continued financial health of the seller/lessee. In most typical transactions, the rental income has been matched up with the buyer's mortgage obligation on the property. Any interruption of lease payments or other shortfall will have to be made up by the buyer.

All too often, sale and leaseback real estate financing is insufficiently analyzed by the purchasing investor. The investor is tempted to think in terms of getting a property for little or nothing because the seller really pays off the mortgage through lease payments. The catch here is that the selling price is inflated and manipulated in excess of the fair market value of the real estate being transferred. If only the seller's business is responsible for the lease, without the seller himself being liable, and the proceeds of the sale go to the seller personally, an even more serious trap can develop. The seller's business might have setbacks or might even go bankrupt. The buyer is still obligated to pay the inflated price to the seller, but there is no rental income to offset the payments unless another tenant can be secured. Therefore, in a sale and leaseback transaction, it is crucial that the buyer be certain that the underlying economics of the sale make it a prudent investment.

When the lease expires, the lessee generally has the option of renewing at a specified rate. The rent is usually set as a lower percentage of the original rent because the building mortgage has been substantially repaid and the costs of ownership and operation are quite low now that most debt service is removed. Sometimes the lease contains a provision giving the seller/lessee the right to repurchase the property for a specified sum. Still, the buyer would not necessarily be unhappy with this--he has enjoyed sheltered income over an extended period and will recoup in a lump sum a portion of the property's value when it is repurchased by the seller/lessee.

The individual real estate investor may resort to a sale and leaseback when he cannot refinance a particular property but needs to raise funds for some other purpose. A corporation that owns real estate and is seeking to raise a sum of money for expansion is another common source for the sale and leaseback transaction. In all events the seller and buyer in a sale and leaseback arrangement must have adequate tax counsel before entering into the transaction, or they run the risk of losing some or all of the tax benefits that make the sale and leaseback desirable.

We shall now work through an example of how to analyze the potential of a sale and leaseback transaction, and compare it to continued ownership and payment of a mortgage.

Let us assume that the XYZ Company owns its plant, which it purchased for $400,000 fifteen years ago. The value of the land was $100,000 and straight-line depreciation has been taken, assuming a 30-year remaining useful life. At the end of 30 years it is assumed that the building will have no residual value. That means that the building was worth $300,000 and each year $10,000 of depreciation may be expensed. The XYZ Company needs money and is considering a mortgage and a sale and leaseback transaction. The mortgage obtainable would be for $500,000 at 12 percent for a term of 15 years. Yearly mortgage payments would be divided between principal and interest as set forth in Figure 8.2 below. Only interest would be a deductible expense, out of the annual level payment of $73,412.

Figure 8.2

MORTGAGE AMORTIZATION

$500,000 PRINCIPAL FOR 15 YEARS AT 12 PERCENT

Year	Principal	Interest	Principal balance
1	13,412.12	60,000.00	486,587.88
2	15,021.57	58,390.55	471,566.31
3	16,824.16	56,587.96	454,742.14
4	18,843.06	54,569.06	435,899.08
5	21,104.23	52,307.89	414,794.85
6	23,636.74	49,775.38	391,158.11
7	26,473.15	46,938.97	364,684.97
8	29,649.92	43,762.20	335,034.04
9	33,207.91	40,204.21	301,827.13
10	37,192.86	36,219.26	264,634.26
11	41,656.01	31,756.11	222,978.25
12	46,654.73	26,757.39	176,323.52
13	52,253.30	21,158.82	124,070.23
14	58,523.69	14,888.43	65,546.54
15	65,546.54	7,865.58	.00
TOTAL	500,000.06	601,181.75	

Annual level payment: $73,412

Now let us say that the XYZ Company can find a buyer for the property at $600,000. The buyer can obtain 15-year financing at 13 percent for the full $600,000 price and offers to rent the plant back to the XYZ Company for 15 years at a yearly rental of $92,845, which amortizes the $600,000 mortgage loan. In this transaction, XYZ Company will lose its $10,000 depreciation deduction and its interest deduction but will gain an expense deduction of all of its $92,845 annual lease payment.

We may now assemble the two alternatives in flow charts and compare their relative merits. The discount factor of 10 percent has been chosen by the XYZ Company to discount each stream of payments and compare the net present value of each alternative. Figure 8.4 shows that the sale and leaseback alternative produces more immediate cash ($540,000 versus $500,000) than a mortgage, and has a net present value above the mortgage alternative of $26,516! (We have assumed that the plant has no residual value at the end of 15 years.)

Ground leases

In a ground lease arrangement, one party owns the land and another party owns the improvements built upon the land. With this technique, investors are sometimes able to finance transactions that would otherwise be impossible to complete if the land had to be purchased. Most ground leases are for a long-term period that matches the expected economic life of the improvements. The ownership of the land is subordinated to the interests of the lender who made the mortgage loan on the improvements. Thus, the lender is paid out first, the developer recoups his costs and realizes a profit on his risk and investment, and then the land and improvements revert to the landowner. The ground lease is another tool for increasing both financial leverage and tax deductions.

Because a ground lease transaction is very complex, most lenders require that leasehold loans be a minimum of $1 million. Protection for the

Figure 8.3

MORTGAGE VERSUS SALE AND LEASEBACK

Mortgage alternative--$500,000 at 12 percent for 15 years

Year	Annual interest	Annual depreciation	Tax advantage @ 48%	Annual mortgage payment	Cash flow	Present value
0	--	--	--	--	--	500,000
1	60,000	10,000	33,600	73,412	(39,812)	(36,193)
2	58,390	10,000	32,827	73,412	(40,585)	(33,539)
3	56,588	10,000	31,962	73,412	(41,450)	(31,141)
4	54,569	10,000	30,993	73,412	(42,419)	(28,972)
5	52,308	10,000	29,908	73,412	(43,504)	(27,012)
6	49,775	10,000	28,692	73,412	(44,720)	(25,244)
7	46,939	10,000	27,331	73,412	(46,081)	(23,649)
8	43,762	10,000	25,806	73,412	(47,606)	(22,208)
9	40,204	10,000	24,098	73,412	(49,314)	(20,914)
10	36,219	10,000	22,185	73,412	(51,227)	(19,748)
11	31,756	10,000	20,043	73,412	(53,369)	(18,706)
12	26,757	10,000	17,643	73,412	(55,769)	(17,768)
13	21,158	10,000	14,956	73,412	(58,456)	(16,935)
14	14,888	10,000	11,946	73,412	(61,466)	(16,184)
15	7,866	10,000	8,576	73,412	(64,836)	(15,521)
					Total net present value of cash flow	$146,266

Sale and leaseback

Year	Annual rental	Annual deduction	Tax advantage @ 48%	Cash flow	Present value
0	--	--	(60,000)	$540,000	$540,000
1	92,845	92,845	44,565	(48,280)	(43,891)
2	92,845	92,845	44,565	(48,280)	(39,899)
3	92,845	92,845	44,565	(48,280)	(36,273)
4	92,845	92,845	44,565	(48,280)	(32,975)
5	92,845	92,845	44,565	(48,280)	(29,977)
6	92,845	92,845	44,565	(48,280)	(27,254)
7	92,845	92,845	44,565	(48,280)	(24,777)
8	92,845	92,845	44,565	(48,280)	(22,523)
9	92,845	92,845	44,565	(48,280)	(20,476)
10	92,845	92,845	44,565	(48,280)	(18,612)
11	92,845	92,845	44,565	(48,280)	(16,922)
12	92,845	92,845	44,565	(48,280)	(15,382)
13	92,845	92,845	44,565	(48,280)	(13,987)
14	92,845	92,845	44,565	(48,280)	(12,712)
15	92,845	92,845	44,565	(48,280)	(11,558)
				Total net present value of cash flow	$172,782

Assumes a capital gains tax at 30 percent on the $200,000 profit at sale but does not account for recapture of depreciation.

lender in a subordinated leasehold transaction is better than in a regular mortgage loan, since security runs to both the building and the land on which no money has been loaned. If the developer fails to meet the mortgage loan payments, the lender may sell both the building and the land to recoup the outstanding balance. As a practical matter, this rarely happens because the owner of the land will make every effort to see that mortgage payments are promptly met (or else the deficiency is advanced) to prevent foreclosure.

For the developer, the ground lease offers an opportunity to make a very highly leveraged transaction. There is no cost for the underlying land in the transaction other than rental payments. Such rental payments, as is the case in a sale and leaseback, are entirely deductible (unlike mortgage payments in which only the interest expense is deductible). For the owner of the land, the attractions are that he receives large rental income when the land is put to use, he avoids the tax on profits that would have to be paid if the land were sold, and in the long term he will benefit from increasing value because the property has been developed for a higher use.

A full discussion of ground leases is beyond the scope of this book. This type of real estate investment is very sophisticated and requires an in-depth knowledge of financing techniques. For now, it is enough for you to be aware that ground leases exist and can be useful once you develop more experience in real estate investment.

Preliminary loan test

There is no single way to be certain that a lender will be willing to finance a real estate investment. Variables such as national market conditions, local economies, size of the project, rapport with the lender, experience, and reputation all play a role. However, if the property is economically viable, your chances of obtaining credit are enhanced. The preliminary loan test set forth in Figure 8.4 below is a handy framework for measuring the project's prospects for gaining the needed financing.

Once you have determined the pretax income of the property you should again work through the worksheet on another basis. Compute the additional debt service the investment would carry if it were financed at the current market rates. To balance the income side you should also increase gross rent by any new rental income you plan to produce, and reduce operating expenses by any savings you expect to incur. If you obtain a positive pretax income in both cases, then things look rather good. These two worksheets will be useful for explaining to a potential lender that the risk of insufficient funds for debt service is improbable in the proposed transaction.

Information needed to obtain a loan

The requirements of lenders vary greatly as to the details they need to ascertain the viability of a particular real estate project. However, to establish your credibility as an experienced investor, it is best to be fully prepared for the most common requests. Over and above this good impression, your creditworthiness will have to stand on its own merits. The three checklists that follow will set forth the general application and closing requirements of some of the largest lenders.

Existing building and land

1. Certificate of occupancy.
2. Year each building was completed.

Figure 8.4

WORKSHEET--PRELIMINARY LOAN TEST

Project: ______________________________

Location: ______________________________

PURCHASE PRICE:

Land	____________
Building	____________
Improvements	____________
Other	____________
TOTAL	____________

EXISTING MORTGAGES:

First mortgage; ______ years ______ mo. @ ______ %
Constant ________
Second mortgage; ______ years ______ mo. @ ______ %
Constant ________

OPERATING INCOME:

Gross rent	____________
Vacancy allowance (present)	____________ %
(A) Gross income	____________

OPERATING EXPENSES:

Air conditioning	____________
Heat	____________
Insurance	____________
Maintenance	____________
Repairs	____________
Taxes	____________
Other	____________
(B) TOTAL	____________

(C) NET OPERATING INCOME (A – B) ____________

DEBT SERVICE:

First mortgage	____________
Second mortgage	____________
(D) TOTAL	____________

PRETAX INCOME (C – D) ____________

3. Two (preferably three) years of operating statements.

4. Three year history of real estate taxes.

5. Detailed rent roll.

6. Cost of purchase.

7. Terms and conditions of the sale.

8. Pro forma statement of income and expenses for the next five years.

9. Description of existing mortgages.

10. Photograph of property.

11. Survey of property.

12. Map of the surrounding community.

Proposed construction loan

1. Survey of land.

2. Detailed description of specific project for which loan is sought and amount of loan.

3. Permanent or standby commitment letter.

4. Personal net worth statement.

5. Bank references.

6. Business references.

7. Pro forma schedule of project.

8. Architect's plans.

9. Feasibility study.

10. Detailed projected costs for each phase of the construction.

11. Terms and conditions of purchase of land.

12. Name and background of the general contractor.

13. A list of permit approvals required and obtained.

14. Future development plans that might affect project.

Permanent loan

1. Description of project.
2. Loan amount, rate, and payout desired.
3. Anticipated construction lender.
4. Personal net worth statement.
5. Bank references.
6. Business references.
7. Detailed projected costs.
8. Name of architect and plans.
9. Copies of any major leases or letters of intent.
10. Feasibility study.
11. Survey.
12. Cost and terms of land acquisition.
13. List of permit approvals required and obtained.
14. Construction schedule.
15. Projected takeout date.

Dealing with lenders

Permanent lenders are institutions that issue the takeout long-term mortgage once a real estate project is completed. Most permanent lenders and construction lenders have floating rates on their loans during the period of construction. This is usually fixed on a prime rate plus points basis to protect the lender in the event there is a large fluctuation in money rates. In recent times, a growing number of permanent lenders have become interested in doing both the construction and the permanent mortgage loan. To induce the developer to lock himself into such an arrangement, without the ability to competitively price permanent financing, some lenders are willing to fix their rates on both the construction portion and the takeout. Using one lending institution for both kinds of financing also has other attractions for the developer. He will only have to pay for one lender attorney, one lender architect, a single appraisal fee, and a single commitment fee.

Many sophisticated lenders have some or all of the following options and conditions required of their borrowers:

1. Lease requirement. A certain percentage of space must have signed leases before the loan is available.

2. Ceiling and floor loan. The loan is for one amount if a high percentage of space is rented and for a lower amount if a lower percentage of space is rented.

3. Estoppel from tenants. The tenants must sign a waiver of claims against the developer before the loan may be taken down.

4. Subordination of tenants. The tenants must agree to subordinate the lease to the mortgagee.

5. Insurance. The lender may require one or more different kinds of insurance, such as completion and fire, for example.

6. Prepayment penalties. Repayment of the loan prior to a certain date will entitle the lender to an additional fee.

Needless to say, it is very important to establish your lending contacts at a main office of the lender and with the highest-echelon officer possible. Don't make the mistake of establishing your credit with those who must have all of your proposals approved by their superiors. You run the risk of having the project explained incorrectly in a second-hand presentation to those with authority, and receiving a negative reply that may not really be justified. On the other hand, it is also wise to try not to step on the toes of subordinates. You should always bear in mind that their boss has to work with them on a daily basis and will try to minimize internal conflicts. This may mean that if you insult his subordinates you would be better off taking your business elsewhere.

CHAPTER NINE

Inspecting and Appraising the Property

A real estate investor must acquire sufficient skill to make a separate, competent, and objective inspection of a property. It is not wise to rely solely on expert appraisers--what you should expect from such professionals is an engineering description and a more or less accurate opinion of present value based on a good faith exchange. The successful investor must build confidence in his own ability to acquire a "feel" for the property and existing buildings in relation to their past use and, more important, their future potential. This does not diminish the utility or the need for professional appraisers. Indeed, your own analysis is a supplementary addition to a sound investment program that includes professional advice. The key to a profit is to move a property and building into its highest use under the circumstances of its location and the market environment for real estate as a whole. Therefore, this chapter will focus on the basic elements of value and how you, as the investor, should be competent to judge them. Since there are so many kinds of real estate investment, not all of these elements will be present in each and every situation.

Lot and location

Usable land, in a desirable location, has become a major cost in new construction. At present, intelligent urban construction cost analysis is allocating 20-35 percent of a project's estimated completion costs to land acquisition. To put that number in perspective, just 10 years ago the cost of land was approximately 10-15 percent of the value of the same type of investment. For example, let's say that 10 years ago an office tower could have been built for a project cost of $50 million. The land under the structure might have had a value of approximately $7.5 million. Today, because of inflation, the same office tower would probably cost $200 million to complete. The cost of the underlying property might well be $70 million. That means that the actual value of the land rose more than 900 percent in the intervening period while the cost of construction rose about 300 percent.

When considering any real estate investment, it is crucial that you walk around the property. Make mental notes on the topography and other characteristics, paying special attention to the following:

1. Sharp changes in elevation in any area.

2. Observe whether grading is away from or toward structures on the property. Rain should run away from a building. If there is a natural rise leading downward to the foundation you might be alerted to the possibility of basement flooding.

3. Small rivers or streams running through a property can be very scenic. At the same time, they could also become a dangerous nuisance. Get a local engineer with experience in water control and management to research potential problems with natural running water.

4. As land in and around urban areas becomes very scarce, marginal property is filled in to allow construction. The type of fill and the method used to locate it on the property must be analyzed. We are familiar with recent cases of fill that had been placed over dangerous chemicals or radioactive materials. The property became worthless as soon as discovery of the problem brought the realization that any buildings on it were unsafe for human occupancy. In less serious circumstances, improper fill may simply cause greatly increased maintenance costs due to rapid and pronounced settling of the foundation, walkways, or parking areas. It's possible to have core samples taken in any filled-in area to determine the type and consistency of the underlying material used for fill.

5. Sometimes land has natural features that make it especially desirable for the particular development an investor is planning. For example, a San Francisco investor planned to construct a suburban hotel. He wanted two levels of parking under the hotel. There was a natural bowl in the area of the site where the structure would be built. An engineer estimated that it would have cost $900,000 for site preparation to recreate that natural excavation.

6. Landscaping is an important element in the overall aesthetics of any property. In a suburban or rural area this means that there should be suitable shrubs and trees to enhance the quality of the buildings on the land. For tract housing development, it is no longer a good idea--if it ever

was--to bulldoze the landscape and build on level but cheerless plots. Smart developers are leaving trees intact whenever possible to increase the value of the individual houses in the development.

In an urban environment, landscaping can mean simply that there is sufficient airspace and light to provide tenants with a pleasant working or living area.

7. Sufficient parking on or near the property is an important consideration. Converting a warehouse to offices or residences is workable only if the size and topography of the plot allows parking for tenants who must travel to their jobs or homes. In an urban area, with a large mass transit system and public parking facilities, it may not be necessary for the plot to accommodate parking.

8. Look for rock outcroppings on vacant land. If you are planning a new structure that requires a basement, remember that the cost of blasting rock can be prohibitive.

As the costs of heating, electricity, and air conditioning continue to rise dramatically, the orientation of a structure on its plot becomes more important. In your inspection, consider the use of the sun's energy to light and warm the building. In winter, in the northern hemisphere, the sun rises in the southeast and sets in the southwest. By midsummer, the sun has changed to a more northerly position, which means more direct sunlight. In colder northern climates, a southern exposure allowing more sunlight into the structure will have a significant impact on the cost of the heating component in operating expenses. Warmer, more southerly areas should preferably have a northern exposure to diminish the sun's rays and thus reduce air conditioning costs.

Walkways, driveways, and parking lots

The surface condition of accessory improvements, such as parking lots and sidewalks, is important. For example, a large parking lot with many uneven depressions can be quite expensive to repair properly. Possibly there was inadequate ground preparation, improper drainage, poor quality fill, or insufficiently thick surfacing material. If you intend to upgrade the building and seek better tenants, pay attention to the parking area. It gives prospective tenants their first impression of the property, and is a daily reminder to the present tenants. Much the same thing can be said for walkways, sidewalks, curbing, and terraces. You don't need to be an expert real estate appraiser to see cracks, uneven joints, and general neglect. Obtain some estimates for repairing defects in walkways, driveways, and parking lots before formulating a bid on the property. Having the facts before you could bring the buyer to reduce the purchase price.

Exterior building inspection

The outer walls of a structure perform many functions. They are an insulation barrier from the elements, they provide strength to the overall structure, and they have an aesthetic dimension that can attract or dissuade potential tenants. If you are making an investment in a property with one or more buildings on it, take time to observe the specifics of the exterior. Look for some of the following:

1. Window sills and trim in rotted condition that will affect their use or require replacement.

2. Drains, downpipes, and gutters hanging loose or otherwise in poor condition.

3. Crumbling of an exterior surface so that it no longer provides an effective barrier from the elements. Be especially suspicious of worn stucco that will need replacement.

4. Cracks in walls and foundations could reflect improper land fill, poor foundation construction, or misuse of the building. The professional inspector should provide some explanation for noticeable cracks.

5. Uneven and patch paint jobs reflect poor preparation and are a sign that the previous owner has failed to maintain the building properly.

6. In a clapboard structure, check for curling or twisting of the boards. They will need to be removed and replaced.

Although it can be difficult to gain access, it's a sound idea to inspect the roof. A visual inspection of drain pipes, risers, aerials, and air-conditioning equipment will give the buyer some idea as to the landlord's control over the tenants and his desire to keep up his property. For example, in an apartment house, aerials and their lines to individual apartments should be securely attached and neatly installed. In a factory or other commercial building, the ventilation equipment and other machinery placed on the roof by tenants should be properly installed and maintained. This means that piping running down the building appears secure, unused or disconnected equipment is removed, and towers are securely fastened to the structure.

The surface of the roof itself is another major factor to consider. There should be adequate drainage to carry off water. If there are patches or soft spots, you might be looking forward to an expensive repair job. If you suspect that might be the case, call a roofer and get an estimate on the cost of restoration or replacement. Try to find out when the last major overhaul was done on the roof; this will be a safe indication of how soon you might have to make a capital investment in roof work, since roof surfaces have limited lifespans.

Insulation

When energy was cheap, it did not matter how well a building withstood the elements. Today, the insulation of a structure is a critical factor in its economic viability. In an apartment house, storm windows are a very important plus in colder climates. General wall and ceiling insulation is important everywhere. It cuts down on noise between units, reduces heating and air conditioning operation, and enhances the value of the property. There are firms all over the country that will do a free or low-cost energy survey of any building. Look for them in the yellow pages of your phone directory or ask the local electric utility public relations department for some names. Don't forget to check on their experience and credentials before relying on their opinions. Such a survey can be worthwhile to the investor, because relatively modest expenditures to upgrade insulation can substantially reduce the cost of energy--and that translates into a solid bottom line.

Interior inspection

The purpose of this chapter is not to turn the average person into an engineer, construction design expert, plumber, electrician, and all around handyman. Nonetheless, your own interior inspection will save you a lot of time and money that would only be wasted for professional inspection and appraisal fees. There are observations any alert layman can make that would force some sort of price negotiation--or even kill the transaction before any money is spent for experts. Here are some of the guidelines successful real estate investors follow during their interior inspection.

1. First, go to the basement and look at the heating and hot water plant. If they look old and the setup feels like Dante's inferno, it probably will need a complete overhaul or replacement. Call in a heating contractor and get an estimate.

2. While in the basement, look at the pipe work. If the large pipes are neatly wrapped and insulated that's a good sign. On the other hand, if they are rusted and corroded, covered with spot patches, and look as if they may leak, it means that soon a plumber is likely to come into your life.

3. The type of piping used in the building is most visible in the basement. Copper and brass piping generally go on forever. Galvanized steel pipe rusts out and clogs in time. Clogging will reduce, and even cut off, water pressure to other areas. If you see galvanized steel pipes, turn on the hot and cold water in every faucet, sink, and toilet in the building. If you don't feel sufficient pressure, be prepared for a large capital expense. Should the investment make sense anyway, then your professional inspector will let you know how extensive the immediate work should be.

4. Look at the electric panels in the basement. Circuit breakers mean that the electric wiring is relatively new. However, older fuse systems may still be adequate. Speak to some of the tenants and ask if they have any problems with electric service.

5. Any stove, refrigerator, dishwasher, or other appliance has only a limited life. Find the model numbers on these appliances and determine what useful life remains, and what their quality was at the time of pur-

chase. If you plan on upgrading an apartment house, new and convenient kitchen appliances attract better tenants. There are discount stores in most urban areas that will sell appliances to landlords at a much lower price than to the public. Locate them and price out what you think may be needed.

6. Each bathroom should have modern and usable fixtures. Look under each sink and toilet to be certain there are shut-off valves. Without such safety devices, a simple broken spindle in a faucet can cause flood damage in large areas of walls, floors, and ceilings.

7. Electric work done by a licensed electrician is always securely attached to the structure and conforms to building codes. If the basement electric work looks like a rack of drying spaghetti, or the wiring in an apartment is exposed and lying on the floor, get an electrician to inspect it.

8. Count the number of electric outlets in each room to be sure they are adequate and convenient for tenant's use. If you see apartments with many extension cords, be alert to the possibility of inadequate service.

9. Look for cracks in walls, ceilings, and foundations. They could indicate that there is extensive settling of the building or some other basic structural problems.

10. Try to open and close some windows. See if they move freely and close tightly to retain heat and air conditioning.

11. Doors that feel flimsy and hollow are cheap doors! Surprised? Of course you aren't. But look at it from the point of view of the potential tenant. Hollow-core doors are probably not safe as entrance doors to apartments or businesses because they are easily penetrated. Also, cheap doors may be a sign that corners were cut during construction.

12. Hallways and other passages should be cheerful, with paint and lighting in good condition. It is oftentimes very expensive to redecorate major hallways.

13. Industrial property must be adequately constructed to meet the needs of the type of tenant you want to attract--loading bays for truckers, heavyweight service elevators for commercial tenants, proper service entries, and the like. You're not an expert on industrial design, so speak to the present tenants and find out their opinion of the adequacy of the building.

14. If you see large amounts of stored chemicals or other unusual materials, make sure the operations of the tenant are in conformity with the local fire code.

Below is Figure 9.1, an Inspection Worksheet that will help you assess a potential real estate investment. It is not designed to cover every possible problem. However, it will help you determine if it is worthwhile to call in a professional inspector and get the complete picture. Following Figure 9.1 is a copy of an actual inspection of an apartment building done by a consulting engineer. It is included here because it will give you an understanding of the depth to which a competent professional can explore the physical nature of a building. This inspection cost $25,000 and took almost four weeks to complete. In a major investment, this is money well spent. There are many grades of inspection below such a detailed report. You have to decide the cost-to-benefit amount that should be spent on a particular property. Inspection fees as low as $75 to $150 are common for a single-family home, while the average 20-unit building will cost about $500 to $1,000 for a thorough inspection.

Figure 9-1

INSPECTION WORKSHEET

1. Property address: ______________________
   ____

2. Broker firm: ______________________
   ____

3. Owner's name: ______________________

4. Pricing:
   a) Total price ______________________
   b) Cash down payment ______________________
   c) Brokerage ______________________

5. Assessed value:
   a) Land ______________________
   b) Building ______________________

6. Zoning: ______________________
   ____

7. Land:
   a) Size of lot sidewalks ______________________
   b) Topography ______________________
   c) Underutilized land area ______________________
   d) Corner location ______________________
   e) Street access ______________________
   f) Plantings ______________________
   g) Parking ______________________
   h) Easements ______________________
   ____

8. Available utilities and services:
   a) Electric ______________________
   b) Garbage collection ______________________
   c) Gas ______________________
   d) Sewer ______________________
   3) Water ______________________

9. General construction:
   a) Brick ______________________
   b) Steel beam ______________________
   c) Cinderblock ______________________
   d) Prefabricated section ______________________
   e) Reinforced concrete ______________________
   f) Stucco ______________________
   g) Wood frame ______________________

h) Other ______

10. Building details:
    a) Date of construction ______
    b) Date of major alteration ______
    c) Date of upgrading ______
    d) Number of stories ______
    e) Approximate square footage ______
    f) Number of rental units ______
    g) Elevators ______
    h) Type of windows ______

11. Description of tenants: ______

______

______

12. Roof:
    a) Construction type ______
    b) Age ______
    c) Condition ______
    d) Type of gutters and leaders ______

13. Plumbing, heating, and air conditioning:
    a) Kind of heating ______
    b) Kind of hot water system ______
    c) Air conditioning method ______
    d) Type of pipes: ______
       i) Galvanized steel ______
       ii) Copper ______
       iii) Brass ______
       iv) Other ______

    e) Major replacements during last 5 years: ______

    ______

    ______

    f) Fire sprinkler system: ______

14. Floor coverings (specify material):
    a) Halls and walkways ______
    b) Kitchens ______
    c) Lobby ______
    d) Other areas ______

15. Amenities:
    a) Terraces ______
    b) Lighting fixtures ______
    c) Stoves ______
    d) Refrigerators ______
    e) Dishwashers ______
    f) Other appliances ______
    g) Washing facilities ______
    h) Pool ______

i) Washrooms ______
   i) Modern toilets and urinals ______
   ii) Washbasins ______

16. Interior walls:
   a) Construction type ______
   b) Painting ______
   c) Cracks ______

17. Foundation:
   a) Basement ______
   b) Signs of water seepage ______
   c) Cracks from settling ______

18. Electrical:
   a) Adequate service for present needs ______
   b) Adequate service for future demand ______

19. Personnel:
   a) Janitor ______
   b) Manager
      i) Agency ______
      ii) Owner ______
   c) Other employees ______

REPORT OF INSPECTION

Re: Apartment Building
Park Avenue
New York, NY

An inspection has been made of the above premises and the following is a report of our findings.

The building is a 20-story apartment building plus penthouse apartments and a full basement. The structure was erected in Lot 12, Block 3, in the Borough of Manhattan, City of New York, in 1968, and is now occupied under Permanent Certificate of Occupancy No. 1628, issued 3/11/70.

The building is classified as Class I fireproof construction and is located in a R-10 zoning district.

1. Site

(a) Location: The above mentioned structure is located on the east side of Park Avenue, between East 72nd and East 73rd Street. Lot size fronts 204' 0" on Park Avenue by 148' 0" deep.

(b) Streets: All streets bounding the structure are public streets paved with asphalt, with concrete curbs. Street lighting is provided by the City of New York and gives good illumination to the front of the building. There is one street light approximately 10' from the main entrance and one on 72nd Street and 73rd Street which illuminates the garage ramp and the Service Entrance.

Street drainage is by the City of New York sewers. Pitch of gutter is sufficient to carry away street runoff.

(c) Drives: There are no drives.

(d) Parking Areas: There is a two level parking garage beneath the building which is run by a parking concession. Parking is available at monthly and daily rates.

(e) Utilities: The building has a combined sanitary and storm drainage system which enters the New York City sewer system. Gas and electric services are provided by Con Edison of New York.

(f) Site Drainage: All site drainage is by gravity into N.Y.C. storm sewers.

(g) Landscaping: Trees are planted approximately every 30 feet in sidewalk tree boxes with iron gratings and decorative steel hoops along 72nd Street and Park Avenue and 73rd Street. There is artificial planting in an area set back at grade under the second floor. There is artificial planting covering exhaust ducts from the garage on the rear courtyard.

(h) Sidewalk: There is a concrete sidewalk at the north, south and west elevation of the building. It is in good condition.

(i) Number of Buildings: There is one building on the site being used as an apartment house, classified as Class A Multiple Dwelling.

2. Building Height

The building is twenty stories high plus penthouse, elevator machine room and tank room. The overall height is 214' 0"±.

3. Occupancy

There are 191 residential apartments having a total of 890 rooms. There are also 17 maids' apartments containing a total of 17 rooms, 1 renting office consisting of 2 rooms, for a grand total of 209 units containing an aggregate of 909 rooms. In addition, there is:

a. Boiler Room
b. Elevator Machine Room
c. A/C Room
d. Tenant Storeroom
e. Workshop
f. Gas & Electric Meter Rooms
g. Tank Room
h. Paint Storage
i. Laundry Room with Toilet
j. Employee's Locker Room with Toilet and Shower
k. Incinerator Room
l. Two Storerooms in Garage Area

4. Violations

(a) Construction Division--none
(b) Housing Division--none
(c) Elevator Division--none
(d) Owner's Registration No. 14520
(e) Building use and floor loadings.

Floor	Live Load	No. of Persons	Occupancy
sub-level	On grd.	10	Garage for 36 motor vehicles and boiler room.
cellar	74 & 120	30	Garage for 33 cars & garage office. Upper part of boiler room, tenants laundry & storage rooms, mechanical equipment room, building work shop, utility room and employees locker room.
first	100 & 40		Building office, mail room & lobby, carriage room & supt.'s office, 2 apartments & ½ apt., 10 maids room & garage office.
second	40	8	8 apts., ½ apt., 5 maids room & sauna (steam room for exclusive use of tenants of this bldg.)
third to twelfth	40		12 apartments each floor.
thirteenth	40		11 apartments each floor.

fourteenth	40	10 apartments each floor.
fifteenth to sixteenth	40	8 apartments each floor.
seventeenth	40	7 apartments each floor.
eighteenth to nineteenth	40	5 apartments & ½ apt., each floor.
Penthouse No. 1	40	4 apartments.
Penthouse No. 2	40	1 apartment & utilities.
Superstructure		Utilities.

NOTE: Garage to be used solely for the storage of passenger motor vehicles of the tenants on premises. Excluded as otherwise provided in Subdivision 1(b) of Section 60 of the Multiple Dwelling Law & Subdivision 9(b) of Section 3 of Zoning Resolution.

Fire Department Approvals:

Sprinkler System August 8, 1969

Standpipe System June 17, 1969

Occupancy

NOTE: This is an amended Certificate of Occupancy to cover cellar and first story changes approved on the present alteration No. 1153.

5. Structural System

The building has a reinforced concrete structural system and fireproof interior partitions. The foundation is reinforced concrete. Subsoil conditions were not available at the time of inspection.

6. Exterior of Building

The building is primarily smooth red jumbo brick from the second to the sixteenth floor which covers columns and spandrels filled in with aluminum and glass store front construction. From the top of spandrel beams to the bottom of windows there is dark green spandrelite. There are two 15' 0" sections of the facade that have white brick accent strips at the spandrels. From the sixteenth floor up, the building is all red jumbo brick. There is a canopy in front to the building that is 9' 0" wide by 8' 0" high by 18' 0" long. The Building Department canopy permit has been issued for the canopy; #MC12/8 expires 5/5/85.

All windows in the building are double hung aluminum with the exception of those above the penthouse roof which are double hung steel. All roofing is gravel and asphalt with the exception of the south penthouse roof which is quarry tile. All roofing is in good condition. Parapet walls are brick with cast concrete cap and all in good condition.

7. Balconies None.

8. Terraces

The following apartments have terraces: 14B, 15B, 16H, G, 17A, H.G., 18F, 19A, F.D.B. Duplex 19, 20E, 1, 2E, and all penthouses. All terraces are red quarry tile with low coping and aluminum rail with enclosed wireglass.

9. Tenant Entrance

Entrance to the building is from grade down a grey flagstone ramp which levels off and then turns left through double leaf stainless steel and glass entrance doors with full side lights of stainless steel and glass. The foyer has a grey flagstone floor enclosed on three sides by stainless steel and glass. The fourth wall houses the apartment communication system. Lobby doors are stainless steel and glass with full glass side lights.

10. Service Entrance

Service deliveries from 73rd Street to first floor service lobby.

11. Roof and Roof Structures

(a) All roofs are asphalt and stone chips with the exception of the south penthouse roofs which are quarry tile. All roofing and roof flashing appears to be in good condition as there are no apparent leaks. Roof drainage is through roof drains, all of which appear to be functioning.

(b) Roof Structures: Housed above the penthouse roof is the house tank, elevator machine room and cooling tower. All are completely enclosed with the exception of the cooling tower which is open to the top and has one wall of open architectural block. All roof structures are in good condition.

12. Fire Escapes

There are no fire escapes.

13. Interior Court

There is an interior court with a quarry tile floor which serves as the roof of the garage below. There is no entrance for the tenants and access can only be gained through the first floor apartment #1E.

14. Other Courts
None.

15. Rear Yard
None.

16. Interior Stairs

There are five interior stairways in the building. Two are limited access fire stairways which run from the penthouse and exit into the lobby. The third stairways run from the basement to the service lobby, and the fourth and fifth stairway runs from the lower and upper level of the gargage and exit onto the street. All stairs are steel with steel risers and concrete treads. All balustrades are steel. The fire standpipe is in the south stairwell with one 50' length of hose at every floor.

17. Elevators

The building is serviced by four Westinghouse elevators and one sidewalk lift. All elevators have V.A.T. floors with wood grained formica walls. The two passenger cars from the lobby have plastic grille ceilings. All elevators are 208 volt, A.C., 13 passenger, 2,000 lb. capacity, and were last inspected on 11/22/80.

Car #26001, passenger service car from basement to penthouse.

Car #26015, service car from basement to penthouse.

Car #26013, passenger service from lobby to penthouse.

Car #26014, passenger service from lobby to penthouse.

The sidewalk lift has a remote station at street level on 72nd Street and runs to a storage room at the garage upper level.

18. Interior Doors
and Frames

The interior apartment doors are wood and frames are metal. All other frames and doors are metal or metal covered.

19. Garage

There is a two level garage on the premises entered from an entrance on 72nd Street. The garage is operated by a concession and is available to tenants and transients on a monthly or daily basis. There are spaces available for sixty-nine cars.

20. Laundry Room

There is one laundry room in the building with six coin operated driers, thirteen washers and two extractors. All concession operated. The driers are power vented to the outside. There is one toilet room off the laundry room.

21. Refuse Disposal

There is a refuse chute door on every floor in the service elevator lobby. The refuse chute runs to the basement incinerator, which is approved by the Department of Air Resources, through the addition of a scrubber.

22. Apartment Schedule

Room	Floor	Base	Walls	Wainscot	Ceiling	Remarks
Living Rm.	Wood	Wood	Plaster	-	Plaster	-
Dining Rm.	Wood	Wood	Plaster	-	Plaster	-
Kitchen	V.A.T.	V.A.T.	Plaster	-	Plaster	-
Baths	Cer.	Cer.	Plaster		Plaster	-
			4'0" C.T.		Plaster	-
	Tile	Tile				
Bedroom	Wood	Wood	Plaster	-	Plaster	-

Bath Fixtures: American Standard

Kitchen Equipment & Cabinets: All kitchen cabinets are wood. Range, dishwasher and refrigerator of varied manufacturer.

23. Schedule of Spaces
Other Than Apartments
First Floor

Room	Floor	Walls	Ceiling	Remarks
Lobby	Flagstone	Exterior glass, others & cols. of mirrored glass & marble.	Ornamental Plaster	-
Service Corridor	V.A.T.	Marble plaster	Exposed-Painted	

Basement	Floor	Walls	Ceiling	Remarks
Boiler Room	Concrete	Exposed Block	Exposed Concrete	-
A.C. Room	"	" "	" "	
Storeroom	"	" "	" "	
Workshop	"	" "	" "	
Motor Rm.	"	" "	" "	
Paint Storage	"	" "	" "	
Laundry	V.A.T.	Glazed Block	" "	
Locker	V.A.T.	" "	" "	
Incinerator	Concrete	Exposed Block	" "	
Storeroom in Garage	"	" "	" "	
Corridors	V.A.T.	Glazed Block	" "	

24. Pest Control

The building is serviced every week by a licensed exterminator.

25. Electrical

There is a 120/208V-3 phase, 4 wire, 2000 amp switchboard (manufactured by Standard Switchboard Company), with six service disconnects.

Service disconnects consist of three (3) 800 amp nonautomatic trip circuit breakers with replaceable Bussman current limiting fuses, two (2) 1200 amp Quick Make-Quick Break switches, and one (1) 1600 amp bolted pressure switches with Bussman current limiting fuses.

The three 800 amp service disconnects feed one (1) meter bank on the Second and Third floors, two (2) on Fifth, Eighth and Eleventh floors, and one (1) on the Fourteenth ansd Seventeenth floors, for a total of 164 apartment meters.

A 1200 A service switch feeds Distribution Panel No. 1 which in turn feeds the Garage Lighting Panel, some motors (all through individual meters) and meter banks on the Fourteenth and Seventeenth floors, for a total of 24 apartment meters.

The 1600 amp service switch feeds a 430HP air conditioning compressor and 1200 A service switch feeds the Owner Distribution Panel. These two switches are on a separate house meter and the current transformer for same and the Owners Distribution Panel are all part of the switchboard on a back to back basis. It was noted that in the Switchboard Room, shelvings have been recently built which have reduced to approximately 24 inches the working space in front of the Switchboard. In addition, there are several fifty gallon oil tanks which are stored in the Switchboard Room.

All of the above are clear violations of Bulletin No. 105-1965 of the City of New York Electrical Code.

The rear door of the Switchboard Room has had its door knob removed, and is blocked by miscellaneous equipment on the mechanical room side. Since this door is required by code as a legal means of egress, it is important that this violation be removed. It is also recommended (although not a violation) that the doors of the Switchboard Room swing out in case of fire.

The Owner Distribution Panel feeds the following: Mechanical Equipment Room Panel, Boiler Room Panel, Fan Room Panel, Laundry Room Panel, Lobby Room Panel, Lighting Panels on the sixth, twelfth and eighteenth floors and the four elevators in the roof elevator Machine Room.

There are eleven meter banks for the apartment panels throughout the building. Each meter bank serves from eight to twelve meters.

Above each meter bank are rows of fusible end lines which feed individual phase 120/240V load centers located around the kitchen area of each apartment. Each load center has a total capacity of 16 single pole 15 or 20 amp mini-circuit breakers.

The building has the following system:

Master T.V. Antenna System as manufactured by Ariel Corp. of Fresh Meadows, New York.

A private intercom sytem with master controls at Lobby-Vestibule location.

Empty conduit telephone system with Telephone Company terminal cabinets located at the first garage level.

In general, all electrical equipment, wiring devices, connections, panels, etc., are in excellent to good condition with the following comments:

Garage:

(1) Exit light fixtures not operative.
(2) 50% of all fluorescent lighting fixtures not operative.
(3) Door alarms not operative.

Exterior Garage Canopy:

(1) Under canopy fluorescent fixture not working and lenses broken.

Apartments: Of all apartments visited, it was noted that adequate numbers of telephone, duplex convenience receptacles and television outlets were provided.

It was noted that the duplex convenience outlet in the living areas were not of the three prong grounding type. In the kitchen, all receptacles were of the grounding type.

26. Plumbing

Domestic water is supplied from the city supply main in street and has a separate meter for the house, the sprinkler system, and the cooling tower. Domestic water is pumped up to enclosed water storage tank on roof by two centrifugal Federal Pumps. From water tank, water down-feeds by gravity and serves all floors.

Water storage tank serves combination fire standpipe and domestic water requirements. Tank has 12,000 gallon capacity with 3500 gallon fire reserve. Tank is automatically filled. Tank and steel supports are in apparent good condition.

One stairwell has fire standpipe system. Each floor has fire hose rack, hose valve, and fifty foot hose. As evidenced by the Fire Department Standpipe Certificate No. 5010, issued 7-29-71, expiring 7-31-74, system conforms to codes.

Hot water is generated in two 2000 gallon storage tanks by steam provided from boilers.

Hot and cold water piping are copper and insulated. Material, water volume and water pressure appear excellent.

Apartment bathrooms contain a combination bathtub and shower, lavatory and water closet. Fixtures are generally in excellent condition and in apparent good operating condition.

Apartment kitchens contain a sink and dishwasher in generally good condition.

Roughing piping for a commercial kitchen is installed in unused basement floor room. Piping is exposed and capped.

Drainage:

The building has a combined sanitary and storm drainage system which empties by gravity into the city sewer in street via a 12" drain pipe and an 8" drain pipe. Soil and waste below the house drain is collected into an injector in the Chiller Room and pumped into the 12" house drain.

Manholes in sidewalk provide access to street sewer connections.

House drain, house sewer, soil stacks, and waste stacks are heavy cast iron.

Roof drains and vent piping are in apparent good condition.

Sprinkler:

Four inch (4") sprinkler connection is provided from city water main in street with valved sidewalk access box. Sprinkler system has water meter, Siamese Hose Connection, and automatic alarm and serves Garage and Paint Storage Room.

As evidenced by the Fire Department Sprinkler Certificate No. 9856, issued 6-15-72, expiring 6-30-80 system conforms to codes.

Incinerator:

Sargent gas fired incinerator with air washer and flue to roof appears in good condition.

Gas:

The gas service is supplied via a 4" diameter feed to building from Con Edison gas main in street to two building meters located in Basement.

Gas serves incinerator, clothes dryers and cooking ranges.

27. Heating, Ventilating & Air Conditioning

The building is heated by two low pressure steam steel boilers (Federal -10,800 MBH each). Boilers have Todd Oil Burners. Steam serves domestic hot water storage tanks, garage unit heaters, and building heat exchangers. All steam condensate return piping is collected in common receiver and pumped back to boilers.

The heating system is being operated under the Department of Air Resources Certificate No. 76/67, which has expired. An application for a new certificate has been filed with the Department of Air Resources in November, 1972.

The number 6 fuel oil system consists of an 18,000 gallon vaulted fuel oil storage tank, two (2) rotary type transfer pumps, and electric heaters. As evidenced by the Fire Department Fuel Oil Certificate No. 2478, issued 9-72, expiring 7-80 system conforms to codes.

Steam to water exchangers produce hot water which is pumped and serves the following equipment:

1) Apartment fan coil units (for winter heating).
2) Apartment Toilet convectors.
3) Vestibule cabinet unit heaters.
4) Heating Coils in Air Handling Units.

The heating and air conditioning system is controlled by summer-winter switch. Winter operation has automatic time clock with outdoor thermostat programming.

Boiler Room has fixed combustion air louver. Some louver blades are broken and in need of repair.

Steam piping, chilled-hot water piping, and vent piping is insulated schedule 40 black steel. Steam condensate return piping is schedule 80 steel. In general, piping and insulation is in good condition.

Snow melting system is provided for building sidewalks. System consists of steam to glycol heat exchanger, circulating pump, and glycol piping under sidewalks.

The building is air conditioned by a Carrier Centrifugal Water Cooled Chiller. Chiller has a 405 B.H.P. compressor, refrigerant R-113, and 430 ton cooling capacity.

As evidenced by the Fire Department Refrigeration F-113 Certificate No. 240, issued 9-72, expiring 8-80, system conforms to codes.

As evidenced by the Fire Department Certificate of Qualification for Refrigerating System Operator No. 204, issued 7-9-70, expiring 7-9-80, the system is being operated by a licensed engineer.

Condenser water is pumped through chiller from Cooling Tower located on roof. Cooling tower is a three cell Marley mechanical draft type. Tower is supported on dunnage beams and concrete piers. Condenser water piping is schedule 40 galvanized steel and uninsulated.

Chilled water is pumped from chiller to Apartment Fan Coil Units in summer operation.

Apartment fan coil units are McQuay Season Maker free standing type. Kitchen fan coil units are manually controlled with speed adjustment.

All other fan coil units have the following features.

1) Return air thermostat
2) Speed control
3) Warm/cool switch
4) Fresh air intake louver.

Chemical treatment for Condenser water system is manually applied.

Air conditioning equipment is generally in excellent condition and in apparent good operating condition.

Ventilation:

Exhaust fans with associated duct work ventilate the following spaces:

1) Interior Corridors
2) Interior Kitchens
3) Interior Toilets
4) Garage
5) Paint Storage Room
6) Studio Apartments
7) Laundry Room
8) Gas Dryers
9) Chiller Room

Some exhaust fans are noisy and in need of repair.

Air Handling Units with associated ductwork supply tempered air to the following spaces:

1) Public Corridors
2) Main Lobby
3) Duplex Apartment

Air Handling Units are in apparent good working condition.

CHAPTER TEN

Real Estate Negotiation

Negotiation is the art of restrained tactical war between parties with opposing individual interests. The buyer and seller, by definition, are each attempting to maximize their position. Each and every concession is won at the expense of the party who made the concession. The idea is to make your concessions relatively unimportant compared to the concessions you gain from your opponent. Skill at negotiating is an essential factor in becoming a successful real estate investor. The bargaining that goes into a real estate contract determines the price to be paid for the property and the terms for its transfer. Price and terms are the two components of profitability.

In all cases, your negotiating strategy should make it appear that any concession is being made grudgingly. You should take the position that each step you take backward must be met with some compensation from the other party. This posture should be maintained even if the item under discussion is of no consequence to you at all. The fact is that your view of the matter is not particularly relevant. The other party considers that point important or he would not have brought it up. Therefore, he should be prepared to concede some other thing to gain your consent. This is the process of trade-offs that brings about a final agreement.

Preparation

A successful negotiator is not necessarily the best orator or debater. The key element to skillful negotiation is preparation. A rundown of the facts, set forth in a sound chronological sequence, is invaluable. Therefore, prepare everything clearly and in writing to avoid the possibility of an impulsive decision being made during an emotional negotiating session.

An age-old method for organizing the facts is a best and worst case analysis. Set forth all of the terms and conditions that you would want in the best of all circumstances; then put down the minimum terms and conditions you would accept if all went badly. Figure 10.1 below will aid you in this process. On the left side is your best case scenario; the right side is the lower limit you will not pass.

Ten rules

A piece of real estate is worth whatever someone is willing to pay for it at the time it is sold. Clearly, the buyer has a slight advantage over the seller because the buyer can determine the limit that he will pay. Past that limit, almost every investment opportunity can be replaced by another one with an equally attractive return. The seller, on the other hand, can only attempt to achieve a target sales price within the financial limits of his potential customers. It is important to recognize the subtle differences in the position of each party in order to be able to capitalize on them. The following 10 rules are helpful hints to negotiation technique when you are either the buyer or the seller. The point of view of each party will reflect negotiating differences.

BUYER

1. Set the maximum price you are willing to pay and stick to it. Don't go in with your maximum on the first offer, because the seller will invariably try to talk you up.

2. Don't discuss your strategy with the broker. The broker earns his fee from the seller and is quite likely to convey everything back to his employer.

3. Try to find out how much the seller paid for the property. If the seller has made a good profit in a relatively short time, he may be more generous with a second mortgage or price concession.

4. Supply the broker with a sales pitch to give to the seller. Point out all flaws without any debate and explain why these flaws make your bid very reasonable.

5. Never, but never, argue with the seller. The seller wants to feel that the buyer is being driven to a hard bargain.

SELLER

1. Set a first offer price and expect to make concessions. Few buyers will accept an opening price, so they expect you to be prepared for a counteroffer.

2. Use the broker to try and get information from the buyer. Most buyers will tell a broker much more about what they are thinking than the buyer will tell the seller directly.

3. Tell the broker specifically to avoid discussions about what you paid for the property and when you acquired it.

4. Take the complaints of flaws the broker conveys from the buyer with a grain of salt.

5. Try to drive the buyer up to his maximum price without losing his interest by petty arguments.

BUYER	SELLER
6. Do not exhibit undue enthusiasm. Let the seller know you appreciate value through your preparation and statements. In tense moments of negotiating, do not suddenly change your attitude and try to become overly friendly.	6. Do not exhibit undue enthusiasm. Make the buyer feel that he is getting a good business deal. Just don't overemphasize the point.
7. Think everything through overnight. Negotiations are tiring and your head will be clearer away from the bargaining table.	7. Same advice.
8. Accommodate the needs of the seller if you can. Cash can be substituted for many of the seller's needs. Be sure to get appropriate concessions in return.	8. Accommodate the buyer--but not to the point of jeopardizing your profits. Get your money out so that it can be used for a new investment opportunity.
9. Try to include expensive improvements in the sale price. Space that is already beautifully decorated and divided is a cost saving.	9. Don't forget about the value of any improvements you have made to the property. Point them out to the buyer.
10. Find out why the seller is selling. There should be a reason that makes sense to you. Dig a little bit to make sure this investment isn't something to pass up.	10. Have a plausible business reason for wanting to sell. No one gives up a good thing without a sensible explanation.

If you recognize the positions of the buyer and seller, it is easier to come closer to your best case position than your worst case position. Where you fall in that range is a matter of skill and technique. The purchaser should try to determine what part of the price can be financed, the cost of such debt service, and the price that makes economic sense. The seller, on the other hand, is likely to be thinking of the taxes he will have to pay on the sale and their consequences to him personally.

Figure 10.1

Negotiation Analysis Worksheet

Topic	Best Case	Worst Case
1. Purchase price		
2. Cash required		
3. Financing		
a) Rate		
b) Term		
c) Constant		
d) Time to get commitment		
e) Seller's second mortgage		
4. Willingness to give deposit		
a) Amount		
b) Conditions		
5. Fixtures included		
6. Closing date		
7. Possession date		
8. Closing expenses		
a) Amount		
b) Who pays		
9. Rights to inspect		
a) Before contract		
b) After contract before closing		
10. Settlement of inspection problems		
a) Correction		
b) Credit to price		
11. Tenants		
a) Lease negotiations		
b) Renewals		
c) Contacting them		
12. Guarantee of rent roll		

Drafting an agreement

Although it is not possible in this book to discuss all of the contractual terms that may be reached in a successful negotiation, there are some basic ingredients of real estate contracts that are commonly present. Below we shall examine some specific contractual provisions that benefit either the buyer or the seller. When the final contract is drawn there will be a balance between the provisions favoring either party, according to the skills each applied to his bargaining position.

1. "Mother Hubbard" clause. It is important to have a true description of the property being conveyed. Sometimes there is more than one description of the property because it consists of several tracts of land. There may also be rights to travel over and use adjoining property. To cover this situation a clause may be added to the effect that the seller is conveying any and all property rights owned at a particular location.

2. Certificate of occupancy. The buyer may ask for a current certificate of occupancy to be sure the buildings are in compliance with local laws.

3. Flood areas. If there is any doubt have the seller warrant that the property is not located in a flood-prone area. (If it is in a flood-prone area, don't buy it.)

4. Brokerage fees. It is not cast in stone that either party to a sale must pay the cost of brokerage. This sum can be a wide-open topic for negotiation, and the contract can specify any division of responsibility for payment.

5. Inspection clause. The purchaser may obtain the right to inspect the property at specified times. Often, the purchaser will negotiate the

right to inspect 48 or fewer hours before closing, to be sure all is in proper order as indicated in the contract of sale.

6. Condition precedent. The purchaser or seller may want a specific event to occur before the obligation becomes fixed. For example, a purchaser may want the town to approve the building of a new road before the contract binds him to the purchase. Likewise, a seller may require that before the purchaser's rights become fixed there must be a third-party guarantee of the purchaser's payments under the contract.

7. Authorization. If the purchaser is a corporation, partnership, or a representative, the seller may want proof of his authority to close the transaction. The form of such proof should be determined by counsel.

8. Survey. An accurate survey can be very expensive and either party can be forced to absorb this expense. It is a point of negotiation.

9. Building permits. The seller may be asked to make the sale conditional on the purchaser obtaining necessary building permits within a specified period of time. The buyer may also pay a set sum to have the seller put the sale at risk during that period.

10. Guarantee. The seller may desire the purchaser to obtain a guarantee of payment by a financially sound and acceptable third party.

11. Risk of loss. Damage to the property after signing of the contract but prior to the closing can be borne by either party. The seller can be obligated to restore the property or may be able to subtract its loss of value from the purchase price.

12. Title report. Who pays for the title report is another item that is open for negotiation. The name of the title company that performs the work is also a matter for discussion.

13. Assignment. A buyer may want the contract of sale to be assignable. The seller will have to agree that such a substitution can be made.

14. "As is" clause. The seller may allow the purchaser ample time to inspect the property to determine whether it meets his investment needs. At that point, the seller may wish an "as is" clause, stating that he is not making any representations or warranties of any kind.

15. Zoning. The seller may be asked to warrant the zoning applicable to the property. Proof of zoning may be in the form of a letter from the local zoning board showing the present zoning classification.

16. Encumbrances. The title report will examine all the encumbrances on the property, such as mortgages, leases, easements, and restrictions of use. How these items affect value is a matter for negotiation.

17. Title insurance. The cost of title insurance is often a major cash expense at closing. Who pays for this insurance is an appropriate item to bargain for.

18. Time of essence. Unless the contract states that time is of the essence, delays of the closing date by the buyer or the seller may be excused. This clause removes all doubt that the closing must be held on a specified date.

19. Purchaser or seller action. Where either party allows the contract to be contingent on something the seller or purchaser must perform, there should be a clause to assure compliance. Such a clause appears where zoning must be changed, plans must be drawn, tests must be made, inspections must be done, or some other matter affecting the property needs to be taken care of before both parties are satisfied. Sometimes such actions can be on a "best efforts" basis.

20. Mortgage assumption. If the purchaser is assuming an assignable mortgage on the property, the specifics should be detailed. The seller may want more money because the purchaser is obtaining financing below the rates currently available in the marketplace.

21. Property taxes. Most contracts provide for the buyer and seller to divide property taxes and certain other items so that each pays what is owed during his period of ownership. This process is called proration and will be discussed below. The seller pays property taxes up to the point of closing, and the buyer returns to the seller any prepaid taxes that extend beyond closing.

22. Oil in tank. There is usually an agreement on who owns the fuel at closing. If the seller owns the fuel, the buyer may have to pay for what is there. This can be quite a substantial item.

23. Leases. The seller should provide an accurate statement about the nature, terms, and conditions of each lease. Try to have this statement in the form of a warranty. Also, find out if the leases have been assigned to other tenants.

24. Utilities. The seller can be asked to warrant that there is adequate water, sewer, and/or electric service available to the property.

25. Inability to convey title. If the seller cannot convey perfect title, the buyer may be able to walk away from the contract or else achieve a reduction in the purchase price.

26. Date, time, and place of closing. These should all be established at the contract stage.

27. Breach remedies. If one or the other party breaches the contract, there remain expenses for attorneys, surveys, title reports, and other

items. These costs can be assigned to either party or the seller can be entitled to keep the deposit as liquidated damages to pay for them.

28. Notice. The method and timing of notice between the parties should be clearly agreed upon. For example, if one party must secure a zoning change, notice of success or failure is important. That party should be required to mail or deliver notice to a specified place in a set time period.

29. Personal liability. The buyer or seller may want personal guarantees on specific parts of the contract.

There is a significant difference between a firm contract of sale with an unconditional obligation to close at a specified date and a contract of sale with negotiated conditions. The seller must be certain that any conditional item is reasonable before he removes the property from the marketplace. A purchaser, on the other hand, will want to include as many conditions as possible to be absolutely certain the real estate investment is safe and suitable. In all cases, conditions should be clear enough that, by objective standards, they can be met. If this is done, a purchaser or seller who knowingly fails to meet a condition within his control will still be under contractual obligation.

Proration

Proration is the division between buyer and seller of the various obligations running with the property. In general, these will be real estate taxes for the current year, school or town taxes for the current year, interest assumed by the buyer, water bills, electricity bills, heating oil remaining in the oil tank, and prepaid insurance premiums.

For real estate taxes and school or town taxes, the process is somewhat involved. In many areas, school or town taxes are paid twice yearly but real estate taxes only once each year. Additionally, the month in which such taxes are due may not coincide with the calendar year. For example, real estate taxes of $1,200 may be due on January 1, and total school taxes of $1,080 may be due in $540 installments on March 1 and September 1. (See Figure 10.2 below.) If a closing is on June 15, it will be necessary to divide the responsibility for these taxes between seller and purchaser. For example, the seller had to pay a full 12 months of real estate taxes ($1,200) on January 1. As of closing, he will have lived there five and a half months and will be entitled to a refund of six and a half months of real estate taxes. Since the monthly cost is $100, the buyer will reimburse the seller $650. School taxes for six months were paid on March 1 in the amount of $540 ($90 per month). Since the seller will have lived in the house three and a half months since then, he will be reimbursed by the buyer in the amount of $225 for school taxes.

Figure 10.2

Real Estate Taxes		School/Town Taxes			Date of Closing			School/Town Taxes			
					15						
Jan.	Feb.	Mar.	Apr.	May	June	July	Aug.	Sept.	Oct.	Nov.	Dec.

Interest and utility bills are usually divided on the basis of information from the mortgagee and the utility company. The buyer's lawyer will check to be certain that all financial responsibilities of the seller that might pass to the buyer are paid in full. If the building has a large tank of oil, the oil is measured and multiplied by the current price per gallon. If there is a large tank (e.g., 5,000 gallons) and it is almost full, a substantial cash outlay may be required at closing. You should get a good idea of the total of these charges before the actual closing. Ask your attorney to furnish a detailed breakdown of anticipated expenses so that there are no large cash surprises.

Title and title reports

Title confers upon the owner of real property the legal right to defend the property against the intrusions of others. The owner wants to be sure of good and marketable title so that any income that can be derived from his investment is secure and for his own benefit. Hidden easements, incorrect zoning, restrictive covenants, and other defects in the deed of a previous owner cast doubt on the quality and security of title. To be fully aware of the condition of title of a particular property, the contract of sale obligates the buyer or the seller to secure a search of the title. A reputable title insurance company searches the public records and discloses any defects that may be present. On the basis of such title searches, title defects are corrected or else a business judgment is made, with the advice of legal counsel, on whether the purchase is still worthwhile. Title insurance is then secured to protect the buyer from all defects in title, except for the items that the title insurance company specifically states it will not insure.

CHAPTER ELEVEN

What Should Be in the Lease?

There is some similarity between the interests of both landlord and tenant in the use of real property. The landlord finds it profitable to permit others to use his property; the tenant finds it beneficial to pay the rent. In other words, both receive some sort of gain inherent in the property or its improvements. The problem we shall examine in this chapter is how to structure the agreement between the landlord and tenant, known as the lease, in such a way that the landlord obtains a proper return on his investment and the tenant derives the maximum amount of use during his occupancy. There must be a contractual arrangement spelling out the rights, duties, and obligations of both parties.

No particular wording or single form of agreement is required by statute in drawing up a valid lease. However, there are some basic factors that must be present in order to transfer the use and possession of real property from one party to another. First, both parties to the lease must have the capacity to make a binding contract. The definition of capacity to agree to a contract varies according to the statutes of different states. Second, there must be a complete and accurate description of the premises to be leased. Third, there must be a specified term for the running of the lease. Fourth, there must be consideration for the lease contract. This means that the landlord will give up his right to use the premises during the term of the lease and receive some sort of compensation from the tenant for doing so. Last, the lease must be executed, delivered, and accepted.

There are six types of commonly used lease agreements. The type depends on the method used to determine the amount of rent to be paid by the tenant. A single lease can contain several different types of rental payments. For example, shopping center leases generally provide a minimum escalated rental payment, as well as a percentage-of-the-gross rental payment.

The six types of common leases are:

1. Fixed rental. The most common type of lease is the fixed rental lease that stipulates a fixed sum of money to be paid on a regular basis during the term of the lease. During an inflationary period, the fixed rental straight lease becomes less popular, because the landlord cannot compensate for rapidly escalating costs.

2. Escalated rental. Many leases today try to anticipate the problems of an inflationary era by adjusting the rental paid by the tenant according to movements in an agreed-upon outside index of changes in a base period of operating costs. Thus, the amount of rent paid by the tenant can be increased during the term of the lease if there are movements in the in-

dex or the cost of operation increases. Some of the standard lease indexes are the wholesale price index and the cost of living index, which are published regularly by the U.S. Department of Commerce, and the Consumer Price Index, which is prepared monthly by the U.S. Bureau of Labor Statistics. There are literally dozens of other indexes that have been agreed upon for escalated rental leases in different areas of the country.

3. Step-up rental. In many cases--the opening of a new store, for example, or the purchase of a business--the tenant can benefit from a reduced rental in the early years of the lease. Over the term of the lease, rent payments step up (increase) until the later years' rent is significantly higher. However, by then the tenant is well established and can bear the cost of increased cost of operations brought on by the higher rental payments. Here, of course, the average rent paid over the entire lease is the key element for both landlord and tenant.

4. Percentage-of-gross rental. The percentage-of-gross lease is very popular in commercial leasing. The exact percentage may vary by business type, location, and size of operation. We have examined this type of lease and some typical percentage rents in our discussion of shopping centers. Percentage-of-gross leases are also common in leasing cropland.

5. Net rental. In a net lease the tenant pays all the operating costs on the property, including real estate taxes, insurance, school taxes, maintenance, and heating. The landlord's role is really limited to the service of the mortgage.

6. Net-net rental. The lease in a net-net rental obligates the tenant to pay mortgage principal and interest costs as well as to pay operating expenses.

From a legal standpoint, there is no limit on the term for which property can be leased. In some cases a tenant may have the right to rent part or all of his leasehold to subtenants. This is legally known as a sandwich leasehold because the original tenant now stands between the landlord and the user of part or all of the property. A sandwich leasehold keeps the original tenant liable in the first instance for the rental payments. Collection of rent from the subtenant is not the responsibility of the landlord but of the lessee.

Commercial leases

A commercial lease is a complicated agreement that requires the advice of competent real estate counsel. Even an experienced real estate investor should not attempt to draft the provisions of a commercial lease. Early on it was suggested that you screen legal advisers carefully. One element you should question is their expertise in the negotiation and writing of commercial leases. Ask to see a copy of a completed commercial lease and read it through. This will serve two purposes--it will give you a good idea of the drafting ability of the lawyer in question, and it will familiarize you with the way in which the points discussed below are reduced to contractual paragraphs in the lease.

Few businesses enjoy the luxury of owning the real estate they occupy. Therefore, rent is an overhead cost of operations and can often be crucial to the success or failure of an enterprise. The landlord wants a commercial tenant who can present a stable business with the ability to meet its rent obligations now and in the future. For this reason, landlords need access to the financial statements of their prospective tenants so that they can evaluate the quality of the applicant.

From the tenant's point of view, the term of the lease and possible options for renewal can be just as important as the amount of rent. If the lease is too short, then it is conceivable that the business might have to move, with the moving costs, disruption of work, loss of customers, and inconvenience that result. Further, the possibility of not being able to locate satisfactory substitute real estate makes it essential for the commercial tenant to negotiate the proper term in the initial lease contract.

As a general rule, the commercial tenant's rent is tax deductible as an expense in the ordinary course of business. The amount that may be deducted in any one year is limited to that year's liability under the terms of the lease. So a tenant who prepays the rent for future years may not deduct the excess over the current year's obligation on his tax return. For example, a tenant whose books are on a calendar-year basis signs a lease on December 1, 1981 and prepays 12 months rent at that date. He may only deduct one month's rent as an expense in 1981 and the remainder of the payment in the following year. In addition to limiting deduction to the tenant's legal liability, the rent under a lease cannot be excessive. If it is excessive, as determined by the Internal Revenue Service, only the reasonable portion may be deducted. As a final note on the tax treatment of commercial rent, keep in mind that many leases require the tenant to pay such obligations as property taxes, school taxes, fire insurance, and maintenance expenses ordinarily paid by the landlord. When this is the case, such payments are considered as part of the rent and are deductible.

The terms of a commercial lease can vary considerably. Whatever the landlord and the tenant agree upon is likely to be enforceable under their signatures on the contract. Some of the most common considerations are:

Parking. Having adequate parking space for employees or customers is a critical business element. In many cases, the landlord will not set aside and designate spaces for the exclusive use of tenants. Such factors as cleaning, lighting, and maintenance of parking facilities are open for negotiation.

Signs and advertising. The tenant may want outside signs on the building or possibly at roadside. To maintain the appearance of the property, a landlord will usually regulate the style and size of such signs.

Personal liability. Where the commercial tenant is not well established or else appears in unsound financial condition, the landlord may seek a personal guarantee.

Sublease. Most leases bar the tenant from subleasing without the express written consent of the landlord.

Purchase option. In a long-term commercial lease where the tenant has made substantial improvements, the lease may grant the tenant the right to purchase the property at a fixed price or at fair market value.

Term. Most commercial leases have a term in the range of fiveto 20 years. However, there is no legal limit on the term of a lease.

Possession. Under many commercial leases the tenant is only given the right to possess the property at the date the lease commences. This means that if the previous tenant holds over beyond his lease the new tenant must take steps to evict him. There can be a compromise position in which the landlord abates rent until possession is obtained or furnishes alternate space acceptable to the new tenant.

Insurance. The tenant is often required to carry fire and extended coverage insurance. Sometimes a landlord may also require rent insurance to be paid by the tenant. This assures the landlord that he will not lose rental income in the event the tenant cannot meet his rent obligation.

Pass-throughs. The problems of inflation and rapidly increasing operating costs have affected commercial lease negotiations. Landlords do not wish to be locked into a set rental, so they pass through to tenants increases in the cost of real estate taxes, fuel charges, utility charges, and other components of operating expenses.

Bankruptcy. Most landlords expressly provide that the lease terminates if the tenant is adjudged bankrupt. Otherwise, the question of the lease will be decided by the trustee in bankruptcy.

Improvements. Many tenants spend substantial sums of money to prepare the rental space for their business use. These improvements increase the value of the property if they are done properly. A landlord will usually require his consent before any alterations are made to the building. Improvements usually revert to the landlord at the termination of the lease.

Surrender of premises. The lease automatically requires a tenant to vacate the premises once the term of his leasehold is up. The lease can provide that when a tenant surrenders the premises, fixtures must be removed and the premises restored to their original condition, except for ordinary wear and tear.

Snow removal. In areas where snow is a problem, the cost of removing it from parking areas, walkways, and entrances is a matter to be covered in the lease.

Use of premises. The permitted uses of the property are important elements of the commercial lease. It is possible to define the range of permitted uses in either a positive or negative way. The positive clause states the actual use of the business in the rented space. For example, "Tenant may operate a shoe store selling shoes in a price range of $15 or more, along with directly related items, such as socks, polish, and shoe-trees." A negative clause specifically prohibits a tenant from using the space for certain business activities. It is common in shopping center leases to see such prohibitions when the landlord is trying to establish a balance of goods and services available to shoppers. However, such restrictive clauses are not always enforceable in court.

Broker's fee. Any brokerage commission should be set out, along with the party responsible for payment.

Tenant's finances. As noted above, many landlords want a yearly financial statement from tenants and the ability to check on such statements. The statement can be used to establish the tenant's ability to pay rent or to compute the percentage rent that may be due under a lease.

Security deposit. The security deposit is intended to ensure that the premises are not damaged and that the tenant will not stay on after the lease has expired. A security deposit is not rental to the landlord and thus is not taxable income.

Renewal options. If a tenant makes improvements to the property, he is likely to want renewal options to protect his investment. A renewal option can be set at a stipulated price in the initial lease, or at a rental to be determined after expiration of the initial term.

Quiet enjoyment. A tenant may request a clause guaranteeing use of the premises without excessive interference from the landlord.

Hours of business. A commercial lease can specify the number of hours and days of the week a business must open. During that period the landlord must provide such services as heat, air conditioning, and elevator.

Assignment. Commercial tenants often request the right to assign the lease without the landlord's consent in the event a business is merged, consolidated, or sold. A landlord can agree to such a provision in the lease, but still require that the assignee assume all obligations of the assignor.

Lease termination

We have previously stated that the law requires no special action to be taken on the last day of a term of a lease. The tenant's leasehold automatically expires. If the lease has been recorded, it is advisable to have the tenant sign and have acknowledged a surrender agreement stating that the lease has ended and he has given up possession. The surrender agreement is then recorded to give public notice that the landlord and tenant no longer have any obligations under the lease. Even if no surrender agreement is executed, the quitting of the premises by the tenant and the re-entry of the landlord is an acceptance by the parties that the lease is ended.

Sometimes, violation of the conditions of a lease may cause the lease to terminate. In an action by the landlord for breach of the lease there are two basic kinds of proceedings. The first is the summary proceeding by which the landlord can fairly readily dispossess the tenant through a rather brief legal process. A summary proceeding is only available for very serious breach of the lease contract, including the failure to pay rent, unlawful use of the premises, when the tenant becomes an adjudged bankrupt, or if the lessee holds over at the expiration of the lease term.

Breach of other provisions of a lease can lead to an ejectment action, which is a more drawn-out affair. The landlord usually has to give the tenant adequate notice of the breach of condition so that the tenant has an opportunity to remedy it. For example, a lease calls for the tenant to install new and proper lighting at his own expense before using certain space. The tenant installs improper and inadequate lighting according to the covenant of the lease. Otherwise, rent and all other obligations are fully and timely met. The landlord would have to notify the tenant that he elects to terminate the lease if the tenant fails to correct the lighting to conform to the standards set forth in the lease. Only if the tenant fails to cure the problem is the landlord likely to bring a successful ejectment action and regain possession of the property.

Sometimes a landlord attempts to harass a tenant into quitting the premises before the term of the lease has expired because he has a tenant willing to pay a higher rent. At other times, a negligent landlord fails to make proper repairs so that some or all of the property cannot be used by the tenant. When the tenant does not have full use of the property according to the terms of the lease, the landlord may have constructively evicted the tenant. In such circumstances, the tenant may be able to quit the premises before the expiration of the lease contract and seek compensation from the landlord for his expenses. It is not constructive eviction when the premises are destroyed through an act of God, such as a fire or flood. In the cases of accidental destruction, most states provide statutes with a variety of possible effects to settle the situation--from rent abatement to the automatic termination of the lease--that will not charge fault to either landlord or tenant.

Residential leases

Unlike the commercial lease, which relates the landlord to a business entity, the residential lease is drawn between a landlord and one or more individuals. Since the premises are to be used for living quarters, there are certain standards that must be built into the agreement to ensure that the parties understand their rights and obligations. The following elements are common contract provisions:

1. Use. The apartment is to be used by the tenant to live in and for no other reason.

2. Security. The tenant gives the landlord a sum of money as security, which will be returned at the end of the lease if the tenant complies with all terms and there is no damage. Interest may or may not be paid on security deposits.

3. Heat, gas, water, and electricity. All utilities must be designated as the responsibility of either the landlord or the tenant. If the landlord absorbs the cost of utilities, the charge is included in the monthly rent.

4. Repairs. Usually the tenant is responsible for keeping all appliances in good order and repair. Failure to do so allows the landlord to make repairs and charge the tenant the cost.

5. Alterations. The landlord almost always requires that his written consent be given before the tenant adds any built-in furniture, railings, wallpaper, or partitions.

6. Liability. The tenant is responsible for all acts of his family, guests, or employees.

7. Inspection. The landlord reserves the right to enter at reason-

able times and on reasonable notice to make repairs or alterations.

8. Bankruptcy. If the tenant files a voluntary bankruptcy petition or there is an involuntary bankruptcy petition filed against the tenant, the lease may be terminated by the landlord.

9. Subordination. All tenant's rights in the leasehold are subordinated to mortgage lender's rights.

10. Landlord cancellation. The landlord may cancel the lease on notice to the tenant that rent is not timely paid, the apartment has been improperly sublet, or the conduct of the tenant interferes with the rights of other tenants.

11. Notices. A place to mail or deliver notices required by the landlord or tenant under the terms of the lease should be provided.

12. Keys. Most residential leases require the tenant to furnish the landlord with a copy of all keys to all locks.

13. Pets. Some landlords allow pets and others do not. This is a matter that should be covered in the lease.

14. Quiet enjoyment. To protect the tenant, most leases specify that the tenant may peaceably occupy and enjoy the apartment for the term of the lease without any conditions that might be dangerous to the tenant's health and safety.

15. Broker's fee. The residential lease should specify if a broker brought about this lease and whether the landlord or tenant must pay a commission.

16. Parking. If parking is available, its cost and location should be specified.

An experienced real estate investor can probably execute his own residential leases without using an attorney. Once the format is established for a particular property, new tenant leases require only the insertion of the term of the lease, amount of rent, amount of security, and several other minor items. For larger buildings, the owner can hire a rental agent who will take care of such details as lease execution.

CHAPTER TWELVE

Management of Property

The ten commandments of management

Management of a building is much like the management of a business. A good manager anticipates potential problems and moves to correct any adverse impact they might have. The term "management" can mean that you perform all of the duties yourself or that you delegate responsibilities to certain hired professionals. You can enhance the profits from your real estate investments by absorbing more and more of the duties that go with them. However, as your real estate portfolio increases, it can become impractical for you to be a jack-of-all-trades. Instead, you are better advised to become the financial expert and relegate the day-to-day operations to others. Here are 10 basic commandments that should serve as a useful guide to landlords in general.

1. Develop a regular maintenance schedule and abide by it. All

physical things have a finite useful life. A building is a collection of materials, which, taken as a whole, provides useful space to the tenant. If you push maintenance far beyond the limits of the building's materials you may create some problems that require expensive repairs. For example, one landlord knew that the gutters and downspouts on his building needed repair and replacement. He decided to let the problem go for one more year. Over the winter, ice formed in an area where the gutters were seriously damaged. When spring brought on a thaw, the resulting water leak ruined the walls in many apartments. This necessitated replastering and repainting a large part of the building. And even if there is no increased physical damage, the tenants are likely to know you're being cheap and become dissatisfied.

2. Ask for personal references. Checking up on personal references is part of your rental homework. There is no guarantee that a personal reference will assure you of a good tenant. On the other hand, if you ask proper questions about character, past and present business, and standing in the community, you can find out a great deal of useful information.

3. Inspect your property regularly. Nothing in the investment or business world functions at its best on an absentee basis. You must make the time to visit your properties and observe how maintenance and other matters are being handled. If you have hired professional managers, you can check on their performance with your tenants. Ask them if everything is satisfactory, even down to minor details.

4. Don't reveal the terms of your property financing to others. The property owner has secured an investment on private terms with a lender. It is not a good idea to let management agents or others in on the exact infor-

mation about your financing package. At some future time, having intimate details in the possession of others may make it difficult to fire professionals who don't perform satisfactory work.

5. Review your insurance coverage every year. In periods of rapid inflation it is crucial that an investor be properly covered on the actual value of the property in case of a disaster. The failure to raise insurance limits can lead to the owner being short of funds to repair damage to the property. This can make your lender nervous and even result in your losing some attractive financing when the loan is called or renegotiated.

6. Treat your superintendent fairly. The first line of contact between the tenant and you as landlord is the superintendent. If you know him personally and have acknowledged the value of his services to you, this is likely to be reflected in his attitude toward tenants. Repairs will proceed more quickly and smoothly, your feedback on the property will be better, and headaches of ownership will be minimized.

7. Keep accurate records of all expenses. When you own property it makes sense to take all the deductions you are properly entitled to. Your accountant will be able to fill you in on the kinds of things for which you should have records. Then it is up to you to get a receipt for each and every expense. One good way of doing this is to open a checking account for each of your properties and pay all bills through the checking account. Then your cancelled check and bank statement provide the necessary records for your accountant.

8. Don't give tenants your home telephone number. For some strange reason, a sane person who would never dream of waking up his doctor at 11:00 P.M., unless it were a life or death matter, feels no remorse about calling

his landlord about a noisy toilet at 2:00 A.M. Get an answering service to screen your calls. Instruct the people at the answering service to contact you if it is an emergency but leave routine matters until the following morning.

9. Stagger the maturity of leases throughout the year. Try not to have several of your leases coming due at the same time. To potential tenants this may be a false signal that there is something wrong with the building when in fact it was just a matter of poor lease planning. When you have several spaces to fill, your property must rely on a greater demand in the marketplace for that type of rental unit. In addition to the staggering of lease maturities, it is also a good idea to try to avoid lease expirations in December, during the coldest months of northern winters, and at holiday periods.

10. Keep abreast of changes in the tax laws and their implications on how you should manage your property. The government comes up with many programs that can benefit you as a property owner. For example, there are energy and other credits to help pay for socially valuable improvements that directly enhance your individual investments. That is the time to spend the money on such subsidized projects. There may also be changes in tax laws affecting how you will be taxed on the sale or exchange of your property. Your lawyer can only advise you on tax law when you have a particular transaction in mind. Plan to gain the best advantage possible from your portfolio by timing changes to coincide with favorable tax treatment. You should keep abreast of the laws through reputable real estate newsletters that can help you formulate long-range management plans. One excellent publication is <u>Real Estate Investing Letter</u>, published monthly by

Harcourt Brace Jovanovich, Inc., 757 Third Avenue, New York, New York 10017.

Modifying the rent roll

The concept behind capital growth is to buy real estate at a present price and develop it to be sold at a higher future price. We have already mentioned that inflation is working in our favor. At the very least, properly selected real estate should keep pace with the inflation shrinkage of invested capital. For the 1980's, an investor should assume that inflation is at least a 10 percent factor. Thus, if you have $50,000 tied up in a $250,000 building, the minimum yearly appreciation should be $5,000. Because of the 5-to-1 leverage factor, this translates into a two percent appreciation on the whole structure. Our two percent is an absolute minimum and in fact an experienced investor should be able to derive five percent or more. That translates into $12,500 of appreciation on $50,000 of cash investment each year.

Basic economic inflation that runs its yearly course is not the only source of appreciation. Investors in real estate can seek out properties that have not been properly maintained or modernized and bring them up to industry standards. As noted in Chapter Two, there are always many real estate investments like this in any area. It requires some imagination and knowledge of construction costs to handle such properties, but the rewards are worthwhile.

For example, you renovate a one-family house. If you can refinance after adding cosmetic changes, you may have acquired a rental property with no cash investment tied up in it.

With apartment buildings, creating additional rental units or space is an art that can pay off by a handsome increase in the rent roll, which translates directly into higher value on the property. In smaller 3- or 4-unit buildings, it is often possible to convert a basement section or garage into a studio rental area. Even in large buildings there are mail rooms, storage rooms, and basement spaces that are potential extra rental units. In office buildings, the location of doorways leading into rental areas can sometimes be shifted to have the tenant pay for what was previously a non-income producing hallway. For an example of this see Figure 12.1 below, where the moving of all doors from point A to point B on each floor added three percent to the total rent roll by removing free space.

Figure 12.1

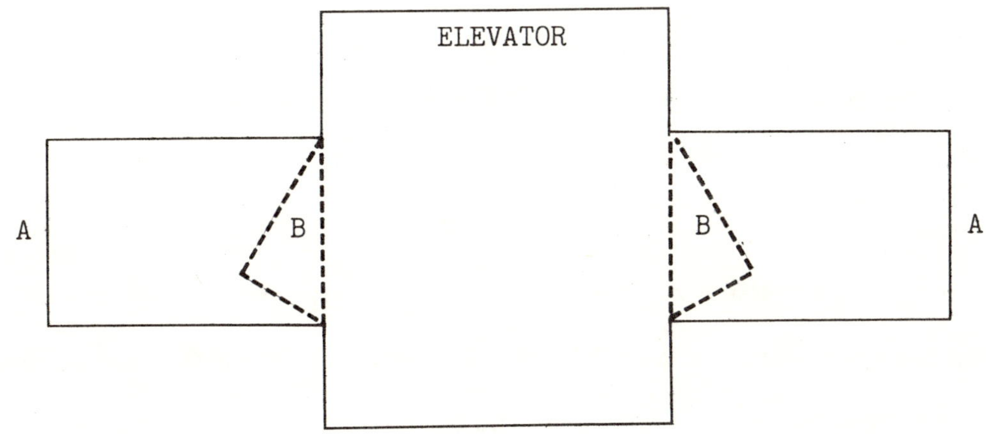

Management guidelines

You should have some idea of the costs associated with delegation of management duties. In addition, there are certain so-called rules of thumb that can help you run your properties profitably. Following is a compendium of such wisdom.

Bookkeeping. A professional bookkeeper should post your real estate income and expenses. Most often this service is available through your accountant. However, it may be cheaper to find a part-time bookkeeper to do the work. Coordinate an independent bookkeeper's method with the needs of your accountant to be sure all bases are covered. Costs for bookkeeping vary, depending on the complexity of the system and the number of properties, but should average out between $10-$25 per hour.

Total expenses. Since the beginning of double-digit inflation and high fuel costs, the percentage of gross income eaten up by operating expenses has climbed dramatically. It used to be thought that total expenses should not exceed 40 percent of gross income. Rents have failed to keep pace with increasing costs, and it is now common to see operating expenses equal 50 to 75 percent of the gross income of a building. Therefore, the investor must judge appreciation potential as well as current income to see if total expenses as a percent of gross income make the property an attractive investment.

Property management. The costs of a managing agent vary widely. There are brokers who are interested in obtaining the listing on the building so they can have the inside track when the property is sold. Such brokers will offer to be a management agent on a break-even basis for three to five percent of the gross income on the property. The problem is that their services are rarely as good as those of a professional management company. Firms that deal almost exclusively in property management generally charge in the range of six to 10 percent of gross income as a fee. The lower end of the scale applies to larger properties where the total dollar amount paid to the manager is high. For a single-family home that you own and are renting, expect to pay around 10 percent or a little more for professional management.

Vacancy allowance. The rule of thumb most property owners use is that the vacancy allowance should be set at five percent of gross income. This should cover the periods in which tenants are changing and also allow for any collection losses. As a practical matter, the central markets have become so tight that most landlords have a much lower vacancy loss. If you are screening the financial ability of commercial tenants carefully, you are unlikely to lose their rent. In the case of residential properties, get a larger security deposit to help offset potential losses. Most tenants try to use their security deposit as their last month's rental payment. For this reason it is a good idea to require one and one-half to two months security before renting. Otherwise you may have to pay for repair of damaged items and bring suit against the previous tenant to collect the cost.

Pets. As a general rule, pets create a real problem for the landlord if they are not properly controlled. They can disturb other tenants, destroy property, and even endanger visitors. An owner should judge whether permitting pets is necessary for a good tenant mix and manage his investments accordingly.

Snow removal. In colder climates it is a good idea to have professional removal of snow from walkways and parking lots. If it is a smaller building, the superintendent can be responsible for this task. The cost of snow removal varies considerably depending on the cost of labor in the area.

Garbage collection. In many areas of the country the landlord is responsible for securing private garbage hauling on a regular basis. Make sure this service is managed properly so that refuse and debris are not a hazard to tenants and a detraction to the property. Replace garbage cans on a regular schedule to keep them functional.

Value to gross rental. The amount you should pay for a property is often figured as a multiple of gross rental. In the hot real-estate markets of Florida and California, multiples of 10-13 times annual gross rental are commonly paid by investors. In other areas of the country, where rent control laws are in effect, this multiple may be reduced to one times annual gross rental. In any case, the message is clear: attempt to increase gross rental if the marketplace will allow it. The higher the gross rental of a property, the more valuable it is likely to be.

Play areas. If you can avoid it, it is a good idea not to have playground areas on your property. Public play areas are better, because they eliminate the threat of a lawsuit against you, as landlord, if a child is injured. If you must have a playground on your property, be sure to inspect it on a regular basis to be certain the equipment is safe and in good repair.

Tenant storage. Landlords who allow tenants to store things outside their rental units should specifically disclaim liability if the stored items are damaged or lost. If you wish to have insurance coverage, the cost may be passed on to the tenant.

Rental owners associations. Membership in a rental owners association can provide a wealth of local experience to help solve routine rental and ownership problems. In most cases the annual dues are nominal. Local associations often have buying contacts for appliances, lighting fixtures, and other items, which make the discount stores seem expensive.

Landscaping. As a rule, gardening expenses should average about two percent of the gross rental receipts, except in years when a major landscaping project has to be undertaken. One of the easiest methods to increase appeal, and probably rental income, of a building is to improve the landscape.

Bonding. It is a good idea, for your own peace of mind, to bond your employees. The value of a bond is as much a psychological deterrent against wrongdoing as a practical protection. It is common knowledge that many bonding companies press charges to the limit to discourage other offenders.

Liability insurance. In today's litigious environment, an owner should carry a substantial amount of liability insurance. Contact a reputable broker, or see if the local rental owners association offers such policies. If a suit is brought against you, it is a good feeling to know that a liability insurer will be acting to defend you.

CHAPTER THIRTEEN

Forms of Real Estate Ownership

In Chapter Three of this book we emphasized the importance of proper tax planning. In Chapter Seven, we explained methods of calculating the expected return on investment of a particular property, utilizing various combinations of borrowings, capital, and operating expenses. This chapter will focus on the ownership form, which is the third leg of a tripod that ties in proper tax planning, ownership, and return on investment. The form under which the real estate is owned should be carefully selected by the individual with his counsel to maximize his specific investment goals. The legal entity holding the real estate determines the amount and nature of the taxes to be paid. This means that in general we should seek a type of ownership that produces long-term capital gains, because of the favorable tax treatment accorded such income. Obviously, the better the tax treatment, the higher the overall return to be received from the investment.

Practical business considerations cannot be ignored in the selection of an ownership entity. We must be aware of the number of individuals involved in the real estate investment, the tax position of the investors, the cost of forming an investment entity, the extent of liability that individual investors will accept, the liquidity desired in the transferability of the investment, and the possible secondary fringe benefits that can be derived by the investors. In the discussion below, we shall touch on the most common forms of ownership and the advantages and disadvantages associated with each form. This discussion sets forth general characteristics that may not be applicable to every investor. Therefore, the use of proper legal and accounting advisers is basic to deciding how to structure ownership of real property.

Corporate ownership

A corporation is a fictitious entity created through special laws permitting it to deal in business and real estate matters in its own name. The corporation is made up of shareholders. Each owns a portion of the total entity directly proportional to the number of shares individually owned as a percentage of all the shares constituting the corporation. It may act in ways that the individual shareholders cannot (for tax or other reasons), and that is its first advantage for the real estate investor. The corporate ownership form is its own taxpayer, investor, borrower, and operator. The state charter, which sets forth the activities in which the corporation will engage, is the only limitation on corporate activities.

Individual shareholders of a corporation are liable for the actions of the entity only to the extent of their investment in it. They are not personally liable for corporate debts or other actions that come as a consequence of the corporation carrying on its business. So the second advantage of a corporate vehicle is limited liability to the extent of the capital contributed to purchase stock.

Corporations are taxed at rates below those of other individual taxpayers. The corporation may retain more of its after-tax profits to use in other investments than can an individual in a high tax bracket. This is the third advantage of a corporation--it may act as a tax shelter by paying taxes at a reduced rate.

Once a corporation is properly created, it can continue indefinitely. It is not dissolved on the death of any of its shareholders, since it is a separate and distinct entity. Thus a fourth advantage of the corporate form is that it functions as long as there are corporate officers with authority to handle the business in which it is engaged. Tied in with continuity, there is the fifth advantage of the high liquidity of corporate ownership. Generally speaking, the shareholders have transferability in their ownership and are free to sell their shares to others. This right may be limited through special provisions against transfer, but such constraints usually arise for a sound business reason at the time of a specific corporate creation. Finally, a sixth advantage of corporate ownership of real estate is that it allows the actual owner the shield of anonymity.

A principal disadvantage of corporate ownership is the double taxation of profit. Income is taxed at the lower corporate tax rates when it is earned. It is then taxed a second time at the individual stockholder level when it is distributed as a dividend. Still, there are ways to draw out income without incurring the double taxation problem. Officers, who may also be stockholders, have the amount of their salaries deducted as a business expense. The individuals pay only a single tax on their personal income tax return. It is also possible to take money out of a corporation by setting up advantageous retirement and pension plans for officer/shareholders.

A second disadvantage of the corporate real estate ownership vehicle involves control. The shareholders vote for various corporate actions, such as the appointment of directors, mergers, and acquisitions, according to their number of shares. Thus, a minority stockholder can be outvoted by the majority of shareholders. This lack of control of corporate destiny can clearly affect his investment; this would not happen in another form of real estate ownership, such as direct individual ownership.

There are other ways in which a corporate charter, bylaws, or shareholder agreement can restrict the action of individual shareholders. Each restriction should be considered for its long-term consequence. Some of the more common restrictive covenants are:

Transferability. There can be a legally enforceable agreement that before a shareholder may transfer his interest, the other shareholders have an option to purchase the shares on the same terms and conditions offered to outsiders. This can create a problem in finding an outsider willing to purchase the shares. The outsider knows that his offer will be accepted only if the other shareholders don't want the shares at his offered price. If the other shareholders don't buy the shares ahead of him, he should ask himself why they didn't jump at the opportunity.

Capital contribution. A stockholder agreement can require additional capital contributions by shareholders on the occurrence of certain events or at a certain period of time. Failure to make such contributions can diminish or wipe out a shareholder's interest in the corporation.

Voting. There are several different methods and actions that can be established to change simple majority voting. All of these methods attempt to exert a particular kind of corporate control. For example, certain stockholders can be given nonvoting stock that becomes voting stock in the event of a specific contingency, such as default on a dividend payment. Or cumulative voting might be required to ensure that minority stockholders have some representation.

In general, a third disadvantage of corporate real estate ownership is the tax treatment of operating losses for the corporation. An operating loss from one property can only be offset by the taxable income from other properties. If the corporation owns only a single real estate investment, then any operating loss is carried over into future tax years to offset future income. Obviously, it would be best for the investor, in the absence of other taxable corporate income, to have the losses used by the individual shareholders in the same year in which they are generated. The shareholders presumably have other income that could be offset by the losses.

One way of bringing this about is through the use of a Subchapter S corporation, which, according to the IRS Code, is taxed as a partnership--that is, no taxes at all are paid on the corporate level. All gains or losses are passed through directly to the shareholders, who may not number more than 15 at the inception of the corporation. (Married couples count as one shareholder.) Any losses are used to offset income, thereby reducing the shareholder's tax basis in his shares. But maintenance of Sub S status is hedged with technicalities, so shareholders should be alert to any changes in the corporate structure that might cause the loss of the Sub S qualification.

As is normal with a tax benefit, there is a corresponding problem. With Subchapter S corporate real estate ownership, the problem is that the corporation may not derive more than 20 percent of its income from passive investment. The rent from residential and commercial property (except hotels, motels, and garages) is considered passive. So you cannot use Subchapter S if you want to buy, sit back, and watch the rent roll in. However, a Subchapter S corporation can actively manage properties, engage in buying and selling properties, or own properties in which the lessor gives substantial services.

Corporate stock that is initially designated as Subchapter S need not continue indefinitely as such. In any future year Subchapter S status may be terminated by the shareholders; the corporation reverts to being a normal corporate entity.

Some real estate investors choose to have each parcel owned by a separate corporation. This will keep the economic and legal problems and benefits of each parcel separate and distinct from each other. The assets of each investment are available to answer the obligations of its own corporation, but not to help pay off debts or unexpected adverse problems of another real estate investment belonging to the group. With many separate corporations, however, it is more difficult to use up losses to offset profits. Also, multiple corporate entities make it more difficult to accumulate a significant amount of income in one place for an investment in a larger property.

Partnerships

A partnership is the association of two or more individuals for the purpose of carrying on a business for a profit. It is a legal entity, just like a corporation, with a registered name under which it operates. Partners contribute capital to fund the partnership in much the same way as shareholders buy stock. Even if the sole business of the partnership is to invest in real estate assets, ownership of a partnership interest is considered personal property just as stock is. However, the conduct of business, individual liability, longevity, and tax treatment of a partnership differ markedly from the corporate procedure.

Partnerships for real estate investment are very popular because they enable several investors to pool their capital and purchase much larger properties on a continuing basis. Each partner will participate in better quality investments as a member of the partnership than he would be able to afford with just his own resources. As we shall discuss below, when a partnership is limited, then the passive limited partners can be insulated from debts and claims against the partnership greater than their equity investment.

The partnership agreement is the basic document spelling out the details of how a partnership will conduct its business. It may provide for the sharing of profits and losses in proportion to partnership interest or describe some other kind of percentage arrangement. Voting rights may also be allocated among the partners in any way that is agreed upon and stipulated in the partnership agreement. Certain partners may receive a return of their investment capital before any distributions are made to other partners. This is common practice when one partner has put up most of the capital and other partners are contributing expertise--the high-risk capital that funded the venture is returned first. Finally, the agreement may restrict the transferability of partnership interests in such a way that it is difficult or impossible to withdraw the capital committed to the investment.

The partners of a general partnership have an unlimited personal liability, jointly and severally, for the debts of the partnership. One partner's acts may legally bind all of the partners and the partnership. That could involve becoming the owner of 100 acres of swampland bought by your partner after a long discussion over four or five drinks. Third parties can rely on the fact that any single partner has such authority to buy or sell property for all the partners. It is possible to create a limited partnership in which some of the partners are considered general partners with unlimited personal liability, while others are limited partners whose liability is limited to the amount of their capital contribution. A limited partnership is something of a hybrid between the corporation and partnership ownership vehicle. General partners manage the daily affairs of the partnership just as officers of a corporation run its day-to-day affairs. Limited partners, much like shareholders in a corporation, have only a minimal role in the active business affairs and decision-making of the partnership.

The duration of a partnership may be fixed at the onset in the partnership agreement, or it may continue at will. However, most partnerships are required to wind up their affairs upon the death, bankruptcy, or withdrawal from the partnership of a partner. A court may also decree the dissolution of a partnership if one partner becomes mentally incompetent and unable to manage his own affairs.

In real estate investments, the partnership-ownership form has several tax advantages over the corporate-ownership form. A partner has his share of partnership income (or loss) passed through to his individual tax return. A partnership's tax returns are filed with the various taxing authorities solely for information purposes. Since real estate often produces tax deductions for items like depreciation, operating costs, interest expense, and maintenance, the partnership may generate an ongoing shelter for other income the individual partner may receive during the year. In the early stages of large real estate projects, operating and start-up costs may include substantial expenditures on commitment fees, loan origination fees, transfer taxes, syndication fees, appraisal fees, and legal fees. There may also be an advantageous investment tax credit for the project. These one-time costs may allow the partnership to show a huge loss for its early operations, which is then passed through to the partners as write-off tax savings worth more than the actual cash put into the partnership.

The Internal Revenue Service will not allow a partnership to pass through losses to its partners if it appears to be more like a corporation than a partnership. Therefore, there are four tests that are routinely applied to each partnership. To qualify for partnership treatment the partnership may not fail more than two of these tests.

1. The partnership should not claim continuity of life. This can easily be taken care of by providing that the partnership agreement terminates upon the death or incompetence of a general partner.

2. A partnership may not have centralized management, because one of

its fundamental characteristics is that the partners have the power to act individually in behalf of all partners. A corporation, on the other hand, has a centralized management function. Limited partnerships fail this test because the general partners act as central management and control the affairs of the passive limited partners.

3. The general partner must have unlimited liability. In other words, a dummy corporation with no assets cannot be made the general partner to give the appearance of unlimited liability. There are rules that require a corporate general partner to have a specific amount of net assets.

4. Participation in the partnership cannot be freely transferable like stock. To ensure that this test is met, the partnership agreement often requires the consent of the general partner, or all other partners, before an interest can be assigned.

If the partnership should fail more than two of the above tests, it will be deemed a corporation by the Internal Revenue Service. This means that it becomes a taxable entity, and can no longer pass through its profits and losses to the partners. When this happens, losses can only be utilized to offset future profits earned by the partnership in its continuing operation.

Joint ventures

There are many real estate projects too large for the resources of a single entrepreneur. The substantial amount of capital required is best spread over several investors. This reduces the risk for each member of the joint venture, yet gives each of them an equity interest in a project that may prove to be successful. Joint ventures are composed of individuals, a combination of individuals and institutions, or in some cases, only institutional participants who pool their staff talents in order to accomplish a specific real estate project.

A joint venture resembles a partnership in a basic sense because it is an association of two or more parties to carry on a business. But a joint venture exists only for a specific project, whereas a partnership is an ongoing association. This means that the individual joint venturers have a different relationship to one another than partners in a partnership. The joint venture agreement is somewhat analogous to a partnership agreement; it spells out how profits and losses are to be divided among the participants. A joint venture agreement also limits the ability of the joint venturers to freely incur liabilities for each other.

For income tax purposes, a joint venture is treated exactly like a partnership. It is not by itself a tax-paying entity, but rather a conduit through which profits and losses from its real estate pass to the individual joint venturers. Thus, the participants in a joint venture may gain some early tax-shelter advantage if there are heavy start-up costs associated with their project. It should be noted here that a joint venture must have the potential for an economic profit and not just generate losses from its investment, or the Internal Revenue Service may decide to treat it like a corporation. The tax-shelter aspect of pass-through losses will thereby be eliminated in the same manner as a partnership that fails more than two of its critical tests.

Some real estate developers promote joint venture projects in which the entire equity in a project is allocated to the backers. The developers hope to make their profit from future management income and up-front selling fees when the joint venture is established. There is a tax reason for this procedure--sometimes the IRS holds that the receipt of an equity interest by a developer, using only investor capital, is really compensation for his services. Thus, the total lump sum value of his equity interest might be immediately treated as ordinary income, a tax disaster. By charging a fee for his services, the developer will only have ordinary income from selling fees and from the management compensation to be received in the future.

One note of caution about syndicated real estate joint ventures. These are real estate investments that are likely to be offered to you by a broker or adviser. Most of what is offered in a readily available syndication is not worth purchasing. Such enterprises are so loaded with front-end costs and ongoing management fees that you will never see a profit. There is little doubt your money could produce much better results through your own efforts in buying, selling, and managing properties. If an experienced real estate investor is participating in a syndicated joint venture, it is probably a transaction involving property he has located himself and is personally sponsoring to friends and family.

Individual ownership

An investor may hold real estate investment in his own name as a sole proprietor. For the conservative real estate investor, individual ownership should be used only for relatively small acquisitions. The corporation, partnership, and joint venture all offer some degree of limited legal liability for the obligations of the investment. In addition, the individual owner adds the net income generated from his holdings to all his other income. This is taxed at the high individual tax rates. Of course, if the property generates a loss, then there is a useful tax shelter aspect that would not be available in regular corporate ownership. So individual ownership may be the only practical and relatively safe tax shelter available to the real estate investor with limited capital.

One reason for acting as a sole proprietor is quite straightforward. Lenders may require the individual to be personally liable for the mortgage instead of issuing it on a nonrecourse basis. This is generally true in the case of purchase and rental of single-family houses, small apartment buildings, or an individual condominium or cooperative unit in a development.

Concurrent ownership

There are three common forms of concurrent ownership that do not involve the creation of a separate legal entity. They are suitable for small projects that involve only a limited group of investors. The three concurrent ownership forms are: joint tenancy, tenancy in common, and tenancy by the entirety.

1. Joint tenancy. The owners of a property held in joint tenancy have rights of survivorship. This means that upon the death of one owner, the other owners receive the right without any payment to the interest of the deceased owner. A joint tenancy can only be created by a specific clause in the conveyance that establishes a joint tenancy relationship among the owners. A joint tenant may not give away his interest by will but is free to sell or give away his interest during his life. When this happens, the joint tenancy is destroyed and the owners become tenants in common. In a joint

tenancy, each owner has income or losses on his individual tax return in proportion to his ownership interest in the property.

2. Tenancy in common. This is a form of ownership in which two or more persons share in the ownership of property on an equal or unequal basis. Each owner has the same right to possession of the property and there is no right of survivorship. This means that any one of the tenants in common may transfer his interest in the property to his heirs by a will. A tenancy in common is presumed in many states where real estate is acquired by two or more persons and there is no agreement to the contrary.

3. Tenancy by the entirety. Married couples can make use of an ownership form similar to a joint tenancy. This ownership form is based on the concept that husband and wife are one. Upon the death of either spouse, his or her interest is automatically transferred to the surviving spouse. Unlike joint tenancy, however, a spouse may not transfer interest in the property without the consent of the other spouse. A divorce converts tenants by the entirety to tenants in common.

Community property

In some states each spouse becomes an equal and concurrent owner of all of the property acquired during the marriage. The theory is that the property ownership is a result of their joint efforts and, absent proof to the contrary, the presumption is that all assets are community property. Property owned before the marriage, received by gift, or inherited through a will is not considered community property, and rents or other income from such property will be owned by the spouse to whom it comes. The income or loss from community property appears on the joint tax return.

Conclusion

It is difficult and sometimes impossible to change ownership forms for real estate once the investment is made. Changing the entity that holds the property can mean paying hefty taxes, although no actual cash income is received. This can drain resources from other investments or even force the unwanted sale of an attractive parcel to avoid having to pay taxes. Experience and good legal and accounting counsel will help you choose correctly, especially if you can provide a detailed write-up of your personal financial situation and the particulars of the contemplated investment. The worksheets in this book are tools that can help you and your advisers arrive at the correct decision.

Good luck in your program for building wealth through conservative real estate investing.

APPENDIX

Cost of Financing

9% ANNUAL PERCENTAGE RATE

	15 YEARS		20 YEARS		25 YEARS		30 YEARS	
AMOUNT FINANCED	MONTHLY PAYMENT	TOTAL FINANCE CHARGE	MONTHLY PAYMENT	TOTAL FINANCE CHARGE	MONTHLY PAYMENT	TOTAL FINANCE CHARGE	MONTHLY PAYMENT	TOTAL FINANCE CHARGE
$10,000	$101	$ 8,257	$ 90	$11,595	$ 84	$15,176	$ 80	$18,969
15,000	152	12,385	135	17,390	126	22,764	121	28,452
20,000	203	16,515	180	23,188	168	30,352	161	37,935
25,000	254	20,643	225	28,986	210	37,940	201	47,418
30,000	304	24,770	270	34,781	252	45,528	241	56,900
35,000	355	28,900	315	40,578	294	53,116	282	66,383
40,000	406	33,028	360	46,376	336	60,704	322	75,866
45,000	456	37,156	405	52,171	378	68,292	362	85,352
50,000	507	41,285	450	57,969	420	75,880	402	94,835

9½% ANNUAL PERCENTAGE RATE

	15 YEARS		20 YEARS		25 YEARS		30 YEARS	
AMOUNT FINANCED	MONTHLY PAYMENT	TOTAL FINANCE CHARGE	MONTHLY PAYMENT	TOTAL FINANCE CHARGE	MONTHLY PAYMENT	TOTAL FINANCE CHARGE	MONTHLY PAYMENT	TOTAL FINANCE CHARGE
$10,000	$104	$ 8,797	$ 93	$12,373	$ 87	$16,211	$ 84	$20,272
15,000	157	13,195	140	18,557	131	24,318	126	30,407
20,000	209	17,593	186	24,743	175	32,422	168	40,545
25,000	261	21,991	233	30,930	218	40,529	210	50,679
30,000	313	26,389	280	37,114	262	48,633	252	60,814
35,000	365	30,786	326	43,300	306	56,740	294	70,948
40,000	418	35,184	373	49,486	349	64,844	336	81,086
45,000	470	39,584	419	55,670	393	72,951	378	91,220
50,000	522	43,982	466	61,857	437	81,055	420	101,355

10% ANNUAL PERCENTAGE RATE								
	15 YEARS		20 YEARS		25 YEARS		30 YEARS	
AMOUNT FINANCED	MONTHLY PAYMENT	TOTAL FINANCE CHARGE	MONTHLY PAYMENT	TOTAL FINANCE CHARGE	MONTHLY PAYMENT	TOTAL FINANCE CHARGE	MONTHLY PAYMENT	TOTAL FINANCE CHARGE
$10,000	$107	$ 9,345	$ 97	$13,162	$ 91	$17,264	$ 88	$21,594
15,000	161	14,016	145	19,742	136	25,893	132	32,390
20,000	215	18,687	193	26,322	182	34,525	176	43,187
25,000	269	23,359	241	32,902	227	43,154	219	53,984
30,000	322	28,030	290	39,482	273	51,786	263	64,781
35,000	376	32,702	338	46,062	318	60,415	307	75,578
40,000	430	37,373	386	52,642	363	69,047	351	86,371
45,000	484	42,044	434	59,222	409	77,676	395	97,168
50,000	537	46,716	483	65,805	454	86,308	439	107,964

10½% ANNUAL PERCENTAGE RATE								
	15 YEARS		20 YEARS		25 YEARS		30 YEARS	
AMOUNT FINANCED	MONTHLY PAYMENT	TOTAL FINANCE CHARGE	MONTHLY PAYMENT	TOTAL FINANCE CHARGE	MONTHLY PAYMENT	TOTAL FINANCE CHARGE	MONTHLY PAYMENT	TOTAL FINANCE CHARGE
$10,000	$111	$ 9,980	$100	$13,952	$ 94	$18,320	$ 92	$12,940
15,000	166	14,835	150	20,928	142	27,480	137	34,410
20,000	221	19,780	200	27,904	189	36,640	183	45,880
25,000	276	24,725	250	34,880	236	45,800	229	57,350
30,000	332	29,670	300	41,856	283	54,960	275	68,820
35,000	387	34,615	349	48,832	330	64,120	320	80,290
40,000	442	39,560	399	55,808	378	73,280	366	91,760
45,000	497	44,505	449	62,784	425	82,440	412	103,230
50,000	553	49,450	499	69,760	472	91,600	458	114,700

11% ANNUAL PERCENTAGE RATE								
	15 YEARS		20 YEARS		25 YEARS		30 YEARS	
AMOUNT FINANCED	MONTHLY PAYMENT	TOTAL FINANCE CHARGE	MONTHLY PAYMENT	TOTAL FINANCE CHARGE	MONTHLY PAYMENT	TOTAL FINANCE CHARGE	MONTHLY PAYMENT	TOTAL FINANCE CHARGE
$10,000	$114	$10,459	$103	$14,733	$ 98	$19,406	$ 95	$24,286
15,000	170	15,688	155	22,159	147	29,106	143	36,426
20,000	227	20,918	206	29,546	196	38,809	190	48,569
25,000	284	26,147	258	36,932	245	48,509	238	60,712
30,000	341	31,376	310	44,318	294	58,212	286	72,852
35,000	398	36,606	361	51,705	343	67,912	333	84,995
40,000	455	41,835	413	59,091	392	77,615	381	97,135
45,000	511	47,065	464	66,478	441	87,318	429	109,278
50,000	568	52,297	516	73,864	490	97,018	476	121,421

11½% ANNUAL PERCENTAGE RATE

	15 YEARS		20 YEARS		25 YEARS		30 YEARS	
AMOUNT FINANCED	MONTHLY PAYMENT	TOTAL FINANCE CHARGE	MONTHLY PAYMENT	TOTAL FINANCE CHARGE	MONTHLY PAYMENT	TOTAL FINANCE CHARGE	MONTHLY PAYMENT	TOTAL FINANCE CHARGE
$10,000	$117	$11,028	$107	$15,596	$102	$20,495	$ 99	$25,651
15,000	175	16,541	160	23,393	152	30,744	149	38,478
20,000	234	22,055	213	31,190	203	40,990	198	51,302
25,000	292	27,569	267	38,986	254	51,236	248	64,129
30,000	350	33,083	320	46,783	305	61,485	297	76,952
35,000	409	38,597	373	54,582	356	71,731	347	89,780
40,000	467	44,110	427	62,379	407	81,977	396	102,603
45,000	526	49,624	480	70,176	457	92,226	446	115,430
50,000	584	55,138	533	77,973	508	102,472	495	128,254

12% ANNUAL PERCENTAGE RATE

	15 YEARS		20 YEARS		25 YEARS		30 YEARS	
AMOUNT FINANCED	MONTHLY PAYMENT	TOTAL FINANCE CHARGE	MONTHLY PAYMENT	TOTAL FINANCE CHARGE	MONTHLY PAYMENT	TOTAL FINANCE CHARGE	MONTHLY PAYMENT	TOTAL FINANCE CHARGE
$10,000	$120	$11,604	$110	$16,426	$105	$21,599	$102	$26,562
15,000	180	17,405	165	24,641	158	32,397	152	39,842
20,000	240	23,207	220	32,853	211	43,195	203	53,120
25,000	300	29,009	275	41,067	263	53,993	254	66,400
30,000	360	34,811	330	49,279	316	64,791	305	79,681
35,000	420	40,611	385	57,494	369	75,589	355	92,962
40,000	480	46,413	440	65,706	421	86,387	406	106,239
45,000	540	52,214	495	73,918	474	97,188	457	119,520
50,000	600	58,016	551	82,132	527	107,986	508	132,801

12½% ANNUAL PERCENTAGE RATE

	15 YEARS		20 YEARS		25 YEARS		30 YEARS	
AMOUNT FINANCED	MONTHLY PAYMENT	TOTAL FINANCE CHARGE	MONTHLY PAYMENT	TOTAL FINANCE CHARGE	MONTHLY PAYMENT	TOTAL FINANCE CHARGE	MONTHLY PAYMENT	TOTAL FINANCE CHARGE
$10,000	$123	$12,187	$114	$17,269	$109	$22,712	$107	$28,423
15,000	185	18,278	170	25,903	164	34,068	160	42,632
20,000	247	24,372	227	34,535	218	45,424	213	58,846
25,000	308	30,465	284	43,170	273	56,777	267	71,055
30,000	370	36,557	341	51,804	327	68,133	320	85,265
35,000	431	42,650	398	60,436	382	79,489	374	99,478
40,000	493	48,742	454	69,070	436	90,845	427	113,688
45,000	555	54,835	511	77,705	491	102,198	480	127,897
50,000	616	60,929	568	86,939	545	113,554	534	142,107

13% ANNUAL PERCENTAGE RATE

	15 YEARS		20 YEARS		25 YEARS		30 YEARS	
AMOUNT FINANCED	MONTHLY PAYMENT	TOTAL FINANCE CHARGE	MONTHLY PAYMENT	TOTAL FINANCE CHARGE	MONTHLY PAYMENT	TOTAL FINANCE CHARGE	MONTHLY PAYMENT	TOTAL FINANCE CHARGE
$10,000	$127	$12,774	$117	$18,118	$113	$23,834	$111	$29,823
15,000	190	19,161	175	27,177	169	35,751	166	44,734
20,000	254	25,548	234	36,236	226	47,668	222	59,646
25,000	317	31,935	292	45,295	282	59,585	277	74,557
30,000	381	38,322	351	54,354	339	71,502	333	89,469
35,000	444	44,709	409	63,413	395	83,419	388	104,380
40,000	508	51,096	468	72,472	452	95,336	444	119,292
45,000	571	57,483	526	81,531	508	107,253	499	134,203
50,000	635	63,870	585	90,590	565	119,170	555	149,115

Source for the following tables: First National Bank of Chicago.

13½% ANNUAL PERCENTAGE RATE

	15 YEARS		20 YEARS		25 YEARS		30 YEARS	
AMOUNT FINANCED	MONTHLY PAYMENT	TOTAL FINANCE CHARGE	MONTHLY PAYMENT	TOTAL FINANCE CHARGE	MONTHLY PAYMENT	TOTAL FINANCE CHARGE	MONTHLY PAYMENT	TOTAL FINANCE CHARGE
$10,000	$130	$13,369	$121	$18,978	$117	$24,968	$115	$31,234
15,000	195	20,053	181	28,467	175	37,452	172	46,851
20,000	260	26,738	242	37,956	234	49,936	230	62,468
25,000	325	33,422	302	47,445	292	62,420	287	78,085
30,000	390	40,107	363	56,934	351	74,904	345	93,702
35,000	455	46,791	423	66,423	409	87,388	402	109,319
40,000	520	53,476	484	75,912	468	99,872	460	124,936
45,000	585	60,160	544	85,401	526	112,356	517	140,553
50,000	650	66,845	605	94,890	585	124,840	575	156,170

14% ANNUAL PERCENTAGE RATE

	15 YEARS		20 YEARS		25 YEARS		30 YEARS	
AMOUNT FINANCED	MONTHLY PAYMENT	TOTAL FINANCE CHARGE	MONTHLY PAYMENT	TOTAL FINANCE CHARGE	MONTHLY PAYMENT	TOTAL FINANCE CHARGE	MONTHLY PAYMENT	TOTAL FINANCE CHARGE
$10,000	$133	$13,970	$124	$19,844	$120	$26,114	$118	$32,656
15,000	199	20,955	186	29,766	180	39,171	177	48,984
20,000	266	27,940	248	39,688	240	52,228	236	65,312
25,000	332	34,925	310	49,610	300	65,285	295	81,640
30,000	398	41,910	372	59,532	360	78,342	354	97,968
35,000	465	48,895	434	69,454	420	91,399	413	114,292
40,000	532	55,880	496	79,376	480	104,456	472	130,624
45,000	598	62,865	558	89,298	540	117,513	531	146,952
50,000	664	69,850	620	99,220	600	130,570	590	163,280

14½% ANNUAL PERCENTAGE RATE								
	15 YEARS		20 YEARS		25 YEARS		30 YEARS	
AMOUNT FINANCED	MONTHLY PAYMENT	TOTAL FINANCE CHARGE	MONTHLY PAYMENT	TOTAL FINANCE CHARGE	MONTHLY PAYMENT	TOTAL FINANCE CHARGE	MONTHLY PAYMENT	TOTAL FINANCE CHARGE
$10,000	$137	$14,579	$128	$20,720	$124	$27,266	$122	$34,086
15,000	205	21,868	192	31,080	186	40,899	183	51,129
20,000	274	29,158	256	41,440	248	54,532	244	68,172
25,000	342	36,477	320	51,800	310	68,165	305	85,215
30,000	410	43,736	384	62,160	372	81,798	366	102,258
35,000	479	51,026	448	72,520	434	95,431	427	119,301
40,000	548	58,316	512	82,880	496	109,064	488	136,344
45,000	616	65,605	576	93,240	558	122,697	549	153,387
50,000	684	72,894	640	103,600	620	136,330	610	170,430

15% ANNUAL PERCENTAGE RATE								
	15 YEARS		20 YEARS		25 YEARS		30 YEARS	
AMOUNT FINANCED	MONTHLY PAYMENT	TOTAL FINANCE CHARGE	MONTHLY PAYMENT	TOTAL FINANCE CHARGE	MONTHLY PAYMENT	TOTAL FINANCE CHARGE	MONTHLY PAYMENT	TOTAL FINANCE CHARGE
$10,000	$140	$15,193	$132	$21,603	$128	$28,424	$126	$35,518
15,000	210	22,789	198	32,404	192	42,636	189	53,277
20,000	280	30,386	264	43,206	256	56,848	252	71,036
25,000	350	37,982	330	54,007	320	71,060	315	88,795
30,000	420	45,578	396	64,808	385	85,272	378	106,554
35,000	490	53,175	462	75,610	448	99,484	441	124,313
40,000	560	60,772	528	86,412	512	113,696	504	142,072
45,000	630	68,368	594	97,213	576	127,908	567	159,831
50,000	700	74,964	660	108,014	640	142,120	630	177,590

15½% ANNUAL PERCENTAGE RATE								
	15 YEARS		20 YEARS		25 YEARS		30 YEARS	
AMOUNT FINANCED	MONTHLY PAYMENT	TOTAL FINANCE CHARGE	MONTHLY PAYMENT	TOTAL FINANCE CHARGE	MONTHLY PAYMENT	TOTAL FINANCE CHARGE	MONTHLY PAYMENT	TOTAL FINANCE CHARGE
$10,000	$143	$15,812	$135	$22,494	$132	$29,591	$130	$36,962
15,000	214	23,718	202	33,741	198	44,386	195	55,443
20,000	286	31,624	270	44,988	264	59,182	260	73,924
25,000	357	39,530	337	56,235	330	73,977	325	92,405
30,000	428	47,436	404	67,482	396	88,772	390	110,886
35,000	500	55,342	472	78,729	462	103,568	455	129,367
40,000	572	63,248	540	89,976	528	118,364	520	147,848
45,000	643	71,154	607	101,223	594	133,159	585	166,329
50,000	714	79,060	674	112,470	660	147,954	650	184,810

16% ANNUAL PERCENTAGE RATE

AMOUNT FINANCED	15 YEARS MONTHLY PAYMENT	15 YEARS TOTAL FINANCE CHARGE	20 YEARS MONTHLY PAYMENT	20 YEARS TOTAL FINANCE CHARGE	25 YEARS MONTHLY PAYMENT	25 YEARS TOTAL FINANCE CHARGE	30 YEARS MONTHLY PAYMENT	30 YEARS TOTAL FINANCE CHARGE
$10,000	$147	$16,437	$139	$23,391	$136	$30,767	$134	$38,413
15,000	220	24,655	208	35,086	204	46,150	201	57,619
20,000	294	32,874	278	46,782	272	61,534	268	76,826
25,000	367	41,092	347	58,477	340	76,917	335	96,032
30,000	440	49,310	416	70,172	408	92,300	402	115,238
35,000	514	57,529	486	81,868	476	107,684	469	134,445
40,000	588	65,748	556	93,564	544	123,068	536	153,652
45,000	661	73,966	625	105,259	612	138,451	603	172,858
50,000	734	82,814	694	116,954	680	153,834	670	192,064

16½% ANNUAL PERCENTAGE RATE

AMOUNT FINANCED	15 YEARS MONTHLY PAYMENT	15 YEARS TOTAL FINANCE CHARGE	20 YEARS MONTHLY PAYMENT	20 YEARS TOTAL FINANCE CHARGE	25 YEARS MONTHLY PAYMENT	25 YEARS TOTAL FINANCE CHARGE	30 YEARS MONTHLY PAYMENT	30 YEARS TOTAL FINANCE CHARGE
$10,000	$150	$17,067	$143	$24,294	$140	$31,946	$139	$39,864
15,000	225	25,600	214	36,441	210	47,919	208	59,796
20,000	300	34,134	286	48,588	280	63,892	278	79,728
25,000	375	42,667	357	60,735	350	79,865	347	99,660
30,000	450	51,200	428	72,882	420	95,838	416	119,592
35,000	525	59,734	500	85,029	490	111,811	486	139,524
40,000	600	68,268	572	97,176	560	127,784	556	159,456
45,000	675	76,801	643	109,323	630	143,757	625	179,388
50,000	750	85,334	714	121,470	700	159,730	694	199,320

17% ANNUAL PERCENTAGE RATE

AMOUNT FINANCED	15 YEARS MONTHLY PAYMENT	15 YEARS TOTAL FINANCE CHARGE	20 YEARS MONTHLY PAYMENT	20 YEARS TOTAL FINANCE CHARGE	25 YEARS MONTHLY PAYMENT	25 YEARS TOTAL FINANCE CHARGE	30 YEARS MONTHLY PAYMENT	30 YEARS TOTAL FINANCE CHARGE
$10,000	$154	$17,702	$147	$25,203	$144	$33,134	$143	$41,325
15,000	231	26,553	220	37,804	216	49,701	214	61,987
20,000	308	35,404	294	50,406	288	66,268	286	82,650
25,000	385	44,255	367	63,007	360	82,835	357	103,312
30,000	462	53,106	440	75,608	432	99,402	428	123,974
35,000	539	61,957	514	88,210	504	115,969	500	144,637
40,000	616	70,808	588	100,812	576	132,536	572	165,300
45,000	693	79,659	661	113,413	648	149,103	643	185,962
50,000	770	88,510	734	126,014	720	165,670	714	206,624

17½% ANNUAL PERCENTAGE RATE

	15 YEARS		20 YEARS		25 YEARS		30 YEARS	
AMOUNT FINANCED	MONTHLY PAYMENT	TOTAL FINANCE CHARGE	MONTHLY PAYMENT	TOTAL FINANCE CHARGE	MONTHLY PAYMENT	TOTAL FINANCE CHARGE	MONTHLY PAYMENT	TOTAL FINANCE CHARGE
$10,000	$157	$18,343	$150	$26,118	$148	$34,325	$147	$42,787
15,000	235	27,514	225	39,175	222	51,487	220	64,180
20,000	314	36,686	300	52,236	296	68,650	294	85,574
25,000	392	45,857	375	65,293	370	85,812	367	106,967
30,000	470	55,028	450	78,350	444	102,974	440	128,360
35,000	549	64,200	525	91,413	518	120,137	514	149,754
40,000	628	73,372	600	104,472	592	137,300	588	171,148
45,000	706	82,543	675	117,531	666	154,462	661	192,541
50,000	784	91,714	750	130,586	740	171,624	734	213,934

18% ANNUAL PERCENTAGE RATE

	15 YEARS		20 YEARS		25 YEARS		30 YEARS	
AMOUNT FINANCED	MONTHLY PAYMENT	TOTAL FINANCE CHARGE	MONTHLY PAYMENT	TOTAL FINANCE CHARGE	MONTHLY PAYMENT	TOTAL FINANCE CHARGE	MONTHLY PAYMENT	TOTAL FINANCE CHARGE
$10,000	$161	$18,987	$154	$27,039	$152	$35,522	$151	$44,256
15,000	241	28,480	231	40,558	228	53,283	226	66,384
20,000	322	37,974	308	54,078	304	71,044	302	88,512
25,000	402	47,467	385	67,597	380	88,805	377	110,640
30,000	482	56,960	462	81,116	456	106,566	452	132,768
35,000	563	66,454	539	94,636	532	124,327	528	154,896
40,000	644	75,948	616	108,156	608	142,088	604	177,024
45,000	724	85,441	693	121,675	684	159,849	679	199,152
50,000	804	94,934	770	135,158	760	177,610	754	221,280

18½% ANNUAL PERCENTAGE RATE

	15 YEARS		20 YEARS		25 YEARS		30 YEARS	
AMOUNT FINANCED	MONTHLY PAYMENT	TOTAL FINANCE CHARGE	MONTHLY PAYMENT	TOTAL FINANCE CHARGE	MONTHLY PAYMENT	TOTAL FINANCE CHARGE	MONTHLY PAYMENT	TOTAL FINANCE CHARGE
$10,000	$165	$19,637	$158	$27,966	$156	$36,725	$155	$45,724
15,000	247	29,455	237	41,949	234	55,087	232	68,586
20,000	330	39,274	316	55,932	312	73,450	310	91,448
25,000	412	49,092	395	69,915	390	91,812	387	114,310
30,000	494	58,910	474	83,898	468	110,174	464	137,172
35,000	577	68,729	553	97,881	546	128,537	542	160,034
40,000	660	78,548	632	111,864	624	146,900	620	182,896
45,000	742	88,366	711	125,847	702	165,262	697	205,758
50,000	824	98,184	790	139,830	780	183,624	774	228,620

19% ANNUAL PERCENTAGE RATE

	15 YEARS		20 YEARS		25 YEARS		30 YEARS	
AMOUNT FINANCED	MONTHLY PAYMENT	TOTAL FINANCE CHARGE	MONTHLY PAYMENT	TOTAL FINANCE CHARGE	MONTHLY PAYMENT	TOTAL FINANCE CHARGE	MONTHLY PAYMENT	TOTAL FINANCE CHARGE
$10,000	$168	$20,292	$162	$28,897	$160	$37,931	$159	$47,200
15,000	252	30,438	243	43,345	240	56,896	238	70,800
20,000	336	40,854	324	57,794	320	75,862	318	94,400
25,000	420	50,730	405	72,242	400	94,827	397	118,000
30,000	504	60,876	486	86,690	480	113,792	476	141,600
35,000	588	71,022	567	101,139	560	132,758	556	165,200
40,000	672	81,168	648	115,588	640	151,724	636	188,800
45,000	756	91,314	729	130,036	720	170,689	715	212,400
50,000	840	101,460	810	144,484	800	189,654	794	236,000

19½% ANNUAL PERCENTAGE RATE

	15 YEARS		20 YEARS		25 YEARS		30 YEARS	
AMOUNT FINANCED	MONTHLY PAYMENT	TOTAL FINANCE CHARGE	MONTHLY PAYMENT	TOTAL FINANCE CHARGE	MONTHLY PAYMENT	TOTAL FINANCE CHARGE	MONTHLY PAYMENT	TOTAL FINANCE CHARGE
$10,000	$172	$20,951	$166	$28,833	$164	$39,140	$163	$48,676
15,000	258	31,426	249	44,749	246	58,710	244	73,014
20,000	344	41,902	332	59,666	328	78,280	326	97,352
25,000	430	52,377	415	74,582	410	97,850	407	121,690
30,000	516	62,852	498	89,498	492	117,420	488	146,028
35,000	602	73,328	581	104,415	574	136,990	570	170,366
40,000	688	83,804	664	119,332	656	156,560	652	194,704
45,000	774	94,279	747	134,248	738	176,130	733	219,042
50,000	860	104,754	830	149,164	820	195,700	814	243,380

20% ANNUAL PERCENTAGE RATE

	15 YEARS		20 YEARS		25 YEARS		30 YEARS	
AMOUNT FINANCED	MONTHLY PAYMENT	TOTAL FINANCE CHARGE	MONTHLY PAYMENT	TOTAL FINANCE CHARGE	MONTHLY PAYMENT	TOTAL FINANCE CHARGE	MONTHLY PAYMENT	TOTAL FINANCE CHARGE
$10,000	$176	$21,613	$170	$30,771	$168	$40,355	$167	$50,156
15,000	264	32,419	255	46,156	252	60,532	250	75,234
20,000	352	43,226	340	61,542	336	80,710	334	100,312
25,000	440	54,032	425	76,927	420	100,887	417	125,390
30,000	528	64,838	510	92,312	504	121,064	500	150,468
35,000	616	75,645	595	107,698	588	141,242	584	175,546
40,000	704	86,452	680	123,084	672	161,420	668	200,624
45,000	792	97,258	765	138,469	756	181,597	751	225,702
50,000	880	108,064	850	153,854	840	201,774	835	250,780

INDEX

INDEX